PERILS OF LIFE

PERILS OF LIFE

TURN LIFE CHALLENGES INTO ETERNAL SUCCESS

LORNA LUMPRIS

CREATION
HOUSE

PERILS OF LIFE by Lorna Lumpris
Published by Creation House
A Charisma Media Company
600 Rinehart Road
Lake Mary, Florida 32746
www.charismamedia.com

Unless otherwise noted, all Scripture quotations are from the Holy Bible, New Living Translation, copyright © 2007. Used by permission of Tyndale House Publishers, Inc., Wheaton, IL 60189. All rights reserved.

Scripture quotations marked KJV are from the King James Version of the Bible.

Scripture quotations marked NIV are from the Holy Bible, New International Version of the Bible. Copyright © 1973, 1978, 1984, International Bible Society. Used by permission.

Scripture quotations marked NKJV are from the New King James Version of the Bible. Copyright © 1979, 1980, 1982 by Thomas Nelson, Inc., publishers. Used by permission.

Design Director: Justin Evans
Cover design by Terry Clifton

Visit the author's website: www.perilsoflife.com

Library of Congress Cataloging-in-Publication Data: 2014910818
International Standard Book Number: 978-1-62136-776-5
E-book International Standard Book Number: 978-1-62136-777-2

While the author has made every effort to provide accurate telephone numbers and Internet addresses at the time of publication, neither the publisher nor the author assumes any responsibility for errors or for changes that occur after publication.

First edition

14 15 16 17 18 — 9 8 7 6 5 4 3 2 1
Printed in Canada

I dedicate this book to my daughter, Kimberly. God has answered my most earnest prayer, that you would develop a personal intimate relationship with Him.

I am very proud of you. Thank you for believing in God's Word. Out of all the blessings you will ever experience in this life, on this earth, this is by far the one that matters most, because it is eternal. It does not get any better than a personal, intimate relationship with our Creator. It is the absolute ultimate.

A legacy of the Word of God is my gift to you.

Love you,
Lorna

CONTENTS

Acknowledgments ix

Introduction xi

Part I: *Perils Steer Our Development*

1   The Bible Is Our Weapon Against Adversity. 1

2   Holy Spirit Is Our Helper 19

3   God Promises to Be the Source for All Our Needs 33

4   The Number One Resource to Conquer Perils 49

Part 2: *Relationships and Surroundings Matter*

5   Order Your Steps 99

6   Be Mindful of Surroundings 112

7   Make Relationship Changes as Needed 121

Part 3: *Surrender in God's Presence*

8   In Surrender God Is Our Companion .129

9   Who Is Leading You? 138

Part 4: *Chart Your Pathway Into Eternity*

10   Discover Your True Journey 153

11   Be Prepared for the End Result 183

Notes 187

About the Author 191

ACKNOWLEDGMENTS

REVELATIONS FROM THE Spirit of God made this project possible. To Him I give all the glory.

I want to express my gratefulness to my friend Margot Murphy, who has been a tremendous blessing and inspiration during this project. She delivered a message from God.

INTRODUCTION

HAVE A MESSAGE to share.

What is the message? God wants to be in relationship with you.

Why would I be interested in the message? Because the alternative is to live a life in sin caused by ignorance to God.

Who is the author of the message? The Creator of the universe. He is knocking on the door of your heart. He desires to fellowship with you. Listen and respond to His life-changing, eternal knock.

Why would I be interested in the message? Because the alternative is to live a life in sin caused by ignorance to God

Why were you chosen to deliver the message? We are all chosen; however, only a few listen and respond.

How did you get the message? Divine discernment.

What is that? When our intimacy with God allows us to hear from Him by way of His Spirit.

Where is the Spirit? It is the innermost part of our being, our heart.

How can I hear the Spirit? We are all spirits who live in a body, so we hear by connecting to God's Spirit.

How do we make that connection? By receiving Jesus Christ as Lord and Savior.

When were you given the message? Early 2011.

Why were you selected to share this message? I pursued God, studied His Word, got to know His ways, and listened for a call.

What do you mean? To know God we must spend time in His Word.

What does this have to do with anything? Our highest priority in the earth's realm is intimacy with our Creator.

What are the benefits? Eternal life and guidance from life's storms.

What kind of storms? The perils of life. Allow me to share.

PART I:
PERILS STEER OUR DEVELOPMENT
Real Tools

THE BIBLE IS OUR WEAPON
AGAINST ADVERSITY

THE BIBLE IS the weapon that adversaries fear the most. No book has incited more opposition or controversy than the Bible. Yet, it has survived every attack with divine discernment, passion, power, and eloquence. The Bible is the only book that contributes to mankind by providing supernatural wisdom on Earth.

Why call the Bible a weapon? A weapon is "any instrument or device used in attack or defense in combat, fighting, or war, as a sword…against an opponent."[1] It is able to do one of two things: either destroy or protect someone based on the circumstance and how we choose to use it. Using the Bible can protect you as well as help you destroy the obstacles that impede your progression in life. One of the most destructive acts of mankind is rebellion against the weapon provided by our Creator. Unfortunately, this rebellion has contributed significantly to man's demise on Earth.

The weapon I reference is the one given to mankind by the Creator of the universe, the Word of God, the sword of the Spirit. The Word is the weapon we must use when we are in the middle of a battle. What battle? Life! Think for a minute. What would happen to a soldier if he were ordered to war in Afghanistan and arrived without a weapon? Would that not be suicidal? Of course it would. The same applies to believers who spend every Sunday in church but are not armed with God's Word. When we don't know God's Word, we don't know how to respond to life's trials and are left defenseless. When trouble arises, our reactions are not aligned with God.

Most of us have a difficult time with the idea that we need to have a relationship with our Creator. But consider this: How do we develop trust with the people in our lives? We try to develop personal relationships with those people. The same principle applies to a relationship with God. We cannot trust someone unless we know them, but too few of us are willing to open up and develop real, healthy relationships with others; hence, most cannot fathom trust in God. Reading the Bible is the most practical way to prepare ourselves with the weapon and simultaneously develop the relationship with God. Unless we cross this bridge and accept that the Bible is the tool for successful living, we will spend our lives in fear and bondage.

Many of us self-destruct. We are ignorant of our most powerful weapon, God's Word: "My people are being destroyed because they don't know me" (Hos. 4:6). One of my most challenging experiences in life brought me closer to God and taught me how to use His Word as a weapon. Ten years ago I was downsized from a lucrative corporate position with a six-figure income. I was a woman of God and of strong faith, but when this life-altering situation happened, I found that I did not have the Word to stand on. At first, I was devastated. I thought of everything one thinks of when they become unemployed. How will I take care of myself, buy food, pay my bills, help my family, live my life, etc.? The devastation and fear sent me on an emotional rollercoaster ride. It was real! I knew that if I did not do something drastic, I was going to self-destruct.

I took the first step. I stopped panicking and, instead, turned to God. I believed in God and that He had a greater plan, so I began to think of my being downsized as being given a promotion from God. I then started the process of my job search, but simultaneously I studied the Bible every day and meditated on God's Word as part of the project. If I was not typing cover letters, sending out resumes, or going on interviews, I was reading His Word, taking notes, and praying on my knees. I immersed myself in the Word so I could arm myself with the tools I needed to survive. I needed to get God's input for divine resolution of my unemployment. My faith never wavered.

I scoured through the Bible to find scriptures to align myself with what God said about the situation. I jotted down all the applicable scriptures and created a list of affirmations to speak and meditate on a daily basis. I read these daily affirmations, while continuing with all the nuances of my job search. I did this for six months—meditating, mailing resumes, praying, networking, reading affirmations, going on interviews, etc. However, no job was in sight. Still, I kept my focus on the Word of God.

At no time did I utter words like, "I will never get a job," or "I am too old for anyone to hire me." "I will lose my home." "I will no longer have a stellar credit rating." "I will run out of money." I knew that those words are all in opposition to what God says. How so? God does not honor unbelief; instead, He honors faith. I knew that standing on my faith was key. In all the time I looked for a job, God always led me to small opportunities that somehow provided whatever I needed. Bills never went unpaid. Thankfully, the Lord gave me the courage to endure. The experience taught me that wavering faith can be disastrous. I would never have survived emotionally without the Word of God.

This ten-year learning process, and the intimate and personal relationship I developed with Jesus, is what I used to propel myself. I am now in the most extraordinary place one could ever endeavor to be in this life.

God's Word always works. Our major responsibility is to follow the guidance and direction of the Bible. God has never failed to deliver on any of His promises outlined in His Word. If you find yourself in a similar situation, try the same process.

1. Don't panic. Instead, put your trust in the Lord.

2. Immerse yourself in the Word.

3. Rest in the assurance that God is in absolute control of your life.

4. Meditate on God's Word.

5. Pray about everything.

6. Beware of the words you speak.

Continue the process until the desired result manifests. Never give up. Stay in the Word, and pray daily.

> Don't worry about anything; instead, pray about everything. Tell God what you need, and thank him for all he has done. Then you will experience God's peace, which exceeds anything we can understand. His peace will guard your hearts and minds as you live in Christ Jesus.
> —PHILIPPIANS 4:6–7

Once you know God's Word on the issue, meditate on the scripture until the Spirit of God provides direction. This process can work in every area of your struggles.

I have studied God's Word and learned that the most effective tool of protection against the darkness and wicked ways of the world in which we live is by the use of the Bible as our weapon. God, in His omniscience, has provided a scripture for every possible life experience. There is absolutely no reason to live in the earthly realm without using the Bible as a weapon for protection. Below are some suggested scriptures for meditation:

> Pay attention, my child, to what I say. Listen carefully. Don't lose sight of my words. Let them penetrate deep within your heart, for they

bring life and radiant health to anyone who discovers their meaning. Above all else, guard your heart, for it affects everything you do.

—PROVERBS 4:20–23

Give your burdens to the LORD, and he will take care of you. He will not permit the godly to slip and fall.

—PSALM 55:22

Look, I have given you authority over all the power of the enemy, and you can walk among snakes and scorpions and crush them.

—LUKE 10:19

As surely as I live, says the LORD, I will do to you the very things I heard you say.

—NUMBERS 14:28

This is my command—be strong and courageous! Do not be afraid or discouraged. For the LORD your God is with you wherever you go.

—JOSHUA 1:9

Commit to the LORD whatever you do, and your plans will succeed.

—PROVERBS 16:3, NIV

The Spirit who lives in you is greater than the spirit who lives in the world.

—1 JOHN 4:4

The tongue has the power of life or death, and those who love it will eat its fruit.

—PROVERBS 18:21, NIV

No eye has seen, no ear has heard, and no mind has imagined what God has prepared for those who love him.

—2 CORINTHIANS 2:9

Delight yourself in the LORD and he will give you the desires of your heart.

—PSALM 37:4, NIV

For nothing is impossible with God.

—LUKE 1:37, NIV

And we are confident that he hears us whenever we ask for anything that pleases him. And since we know he hears us when we make our requests, we also know that he will give us what we ask for.

—1 John 5:14–15

Trust in the LORD with all your heart; do not depend on your own understanding. Seek his will in all you do, and he will show you which path to take.

—PROVERBS 3:5–6

I have experienced the peril of unemployment and remained in an absolute surrender to God. Although it was very difficult at times, I stayed in faith to the Word of God. After the second year of being unemployed, I knew it was not coincidental and that the situation was way bigger than me. God was determined to get my attention. As I later learned, God had a plan for me. God's plans are so much greater than what our puny minds can conceive. Because I was listening, when the assignment came to me from God to write a book, I was able to receive it. Although initially I felt very unqualified for the job, I embraced it. I knew God was more than qualified than I and that with Him I could do anything.

Do you have an intimate, personal relationship with your Creator? God has an assignment for you. Are you prepared to receive it? The pursuit of a relationship with Jesus Christ is the key to receive your godly assignment. Make a correction now and give God the attention He deserves. Do not wait until He takes it by force, for it is very painful.

Oh, foolish Galatians! Who has cast an evil spell on you? For the meaning of Jesus Christ's death was made as clear to you as if you had seen a picture of his death on the cross. Let me ask you this one question: Did you receive the Holy Spirit by obeying the law of Moses? Of course not! You received the Spirit because you believed the message you heard about Christ.

—GALATIANS 3:1–2

THE BIBLE AS A FOUNDATION FOR EVERYTHING

Our Creator's intent for humanity was for us to experience an intimate, personal relationship with Him. The only way to accomplish this successfully is with the guidance and direction of the Holy Spirit. Although this is not an easy task, it is one worth striving to accomplish.

When I first started to study the Word of God, I was led to read the Book of Proverbs. Proverbs contains practical instructions for successful living and teaches about a special wisdom revealed by God. Both must play a part in our daily lives. The Book of Proverbs covers a range of topics, from discipline of children to social justice, foolish talk, and money. The basic theme of the book is that fear of the Lord is the beginning of knowledge. Our human wisdom is great and necessary. However, no matter how skilled we are, without a humble willingness to learn from God, we will certainly end up in trouble.

The Book of Proverbs has thirty-one chapters. Since there are essentially the same number of days in a calendar month, I read a chapter a day from The Living Bible, starting from the beginning of the month, and repeated this process over and over every month for six months. This synchronization aligned quite nicely with my strategy and made it easy to be consistent. Additionally, since faith comes by hearing, and hearing by the Word of God (Rom. 10:17, KJV), I felt the repetition of scriptures would put me on the right track to develop my faith. I chose The Living Bible because, in my opinion, it is the easiest to understand.

I noticed that after this six-month period, the Spirit of God began leading me to other areas of the Bible. I also noticed that I no longer had an interest in participating in activities that distracted me from my spiritual journey. For example, I lost interest in watching television and engaging in social media activities. Ridding my world of distractions allowed the Word of God to renew my mind. My intimacy with God became my highest priority. I believe that my concentration and pursuit of the relationship led to a life-changing supernatural experience.

In March of 2006 I had what I can best describe as a visitation from the Spirit of God. I will share the experience as best as I am able. Although, this was something I would have never imagined in my wildest dreams, there is a scripture in the Bible that best describes the episode: "No eye has seen, no ear has heard, and no mind has imagined what God has prepared for those who love him" (1 Cor. 2:9).

My expectation for great things has always hovered around the level of extraordinary, because I have faith in God's Word. However, this occurrence was way beyond any such expectation. One particular night in March 2006, I went to bed as I would any other night. However, at approximately 2:00 a.m., I was awakened by a burst of brightness in my bedroom. When I opened my eyes, the Spirit of God stood above me, hovering about the ceiling. I was in utter shock and astonished by what I was seeing, but I was not afraid. All that surrounded the Spirit was one of the most beautiful places my eyes had ever seen. I saw beautiful colors like deep red; electric blue; bright, sun-like yellow; and pristine green grass in the midst of a meadow. Then I heard the words that were coming from within my spirit: "I am your Source, and everything comes through me and from me." Then the vision was gone. It was a very short encounter. I would say the first part lasted approximately one minute.

The vision then left and was back about two minutes later and stayed for about the same amount of time. The time span was more than enough for God to get my undivided attention. I immediately got out of bed and wrote down everything that happened in my journal. Just imagine being jobless, at the lowest point in your life, and the Spirit of God shows up in your bedroom and provides assurance that He is with you! When I received this revelation of the truth of God, it changed my entire perspective of my purpose on Earth.

After this encounter I immersed myself completely in the Word of God. I so enjoy my alone time in communion with the Spirit of God within. It is the most joyous experience of my life. Sometimes I just burst into tears—not tears of sadness but of joy of the Lord. What comes to mind during these moments is, "Oh, Lord, thank You for discipline. Had I not gone through the life-altering experience of being downsized, I would have continued in my ignorance from fear and bondage in the world system." Since the visitation in 2006, God continues to provide me with discernment and revelations.

I was meditating one day and thought to myself, if I was able to trust an employer, a mere human being, for a paycheck and my livelihood, why not put my trust in God, Creator of all things? As I continued to study God's Word, I aligned myself with its teachings. What I learned during this experience is that all along I was not alone, but I was walking with God. The Lord is with me all the time—every second, every minute, and every hour of each day. All He requires is obedience and trust in Him.

> Now glory be to God! By this mighty power at work within us, he
> is able to accomplish infinitely more than we would ever dare to
> ask or hope.
> —Ephesians 3:20

Authorized to Use the Bible as a Weapon

Who are those authorized to use the Bible as weapon? All of Earth's population! All that is required for us to arm ourselves with the Word of God is desire, acceptance, and belief. For anyone unfamiliar with this concept, this is what Jesus said: "Most assuredly, I say to you, unless one is born of water and the Spirit, he cannot enter the kingdom of God" (John 3:5,

NKJV). John 3 tells of the story when Nicodemus, a Pharisee, went to speak with Jesus. Nicodemus had the same question as many others: How does a grown person become born again? He said, "Teacher…we all know that God has sent you to teach us. Your miraculous signs are proof enough that God is with you" (v. 2). Nicodemus, very perplexed, asked Jesus, "How can an old man go back into his mother's womb and be born again?" (v. 4). Jesus replied, "The truth is, no one can enter the Kingdom of God without being born of water and the Spirit. Humans can reproduce only human life, but the Holy Spirit gives new life from heaven" (vv. 5–6). The Spirit of God is the only Teacher that could bring this revelation to the forefront in the lives of those who believe. All we need to do is confess with our mouths and believe in our hearts that Jesus is the Son of God and that He died on the cross to save us, and access is granted.

> So I advise you to live according to your new life in the Holy Spirit. Then you won't be doing what your sinful nature craves. The old sinful nature loves to do evil, which is just opposite from what the Holy Spirit wants.
> —GALATIANS 5:16–17

As a Christian, like most believers, I attended church regularly for most of my life. However, God's Word was not the final authority in my life until ten years ago. It is very regrettable that most of us only seek to hear from God when we have an unfortunate situation in our lives, and when that has been corrected, we go back to our old way of being. I discovered the Bible as a weapon only after much pain and heartbreak. I am now in an incessant pursuit to be in relation with our Creator. The revelation would not have been so clear without my pursuit and passion for knowledge. Had I not discovered this truth, I would have continued a life of ignorance, hidden from God's Word.

EFFECTIVE USE OF THE WEAPON

The Bible is the resource for protection for everything placed in our path. Scripture tells us:

> Put on all of God's armor so that you will be able to stand firm against all strategies and tricks of the Devil. For we are not fighting against people made of flesh and blood, but against the evil rulers and authorities of the unseen world, against those mighty powers of darkness who rule this world, and against wicked spirits in the heavenly realms. Use every piece of God's armor to resist the enemy

in the time of evil, so that after the battle you will still be standing firm. Stand your ground, putting on the sturdy belt of truth and the body armor of God's righteousness. For shoes, put on the peace that comes from the Good News, so that you will be fully prepared. In every battle you will need faith as your shield to stop the fiery arrows aimed at you by Satan. Put on salvation as your helmet, and take the sword of the Spirit, which is the word of God.

—EPHESIANS 6:11–17

Always maintain access to the Word of God for protection against the evil of the world. Every day, believers are required to grapple with obstacles that hinder communication with God. This causes us to struggle not with God but with the things that might cause us to disobey Him. One of the major causes of disobedience to the Word of God is greed, the appetite that always whispers, "Take it now, never later." People inherently want to satisfy themselves first rather than God. One of the ways we can effectively serve God is by using His Word to enlighten non-believers and enhancing the lives of other believers by sharing our knowledge. Serving God is a day-to-day commitment.

Five years ago I joined a church where I believe I was led by God. On my first visit to the church I was provided with an index card to fill out my contact information. Approximately a week later I received a call from the pastor, asking if she could visit me at home. My response was, "Absolutely," and she stopped by the following day. In our conversation I mentioned that I was interested in teaching a Bible study to the high school student members of the church. The pastor accepted, and I was delighted to serve. My first youth Bible study lesson was scheduled a month later. By then, I had been so immersed in the Word for about five years that I was excited to share my knowledge. In hindsight, the reason I wanted to share was because I wanted to give the students something I never had.

Bible study was nonexistent in my childhood Christian education. In my early Sunday school years there was no teacher or teaching that stood out, and no one with a passion for God or His Word to guide my siblings and me in this journey called life. To be honest, I had never met a Christian leader who emulated the extraordinariness of "the Jesus within" while I was growing up. Not even my parents. Although attending church was mandatory in our home, my parents did not study the Bible. It was not until I was an adult that I received the true revelation of the Spirit of God within. That was truly an eye opener. What I missed by not learning to use the Bible as my guide through life was what I now believe to be the most important part of any child's upbringing. I am committed that the legacy of not teaching the Word of God to our children will not be repeated on my watch. The most important part of raising a child is to teach them how to use the Word of God, "the sword of the Spirit"

As parents, many of us have stolen this heavenly inheritance of our children. We train our children to do so many tasks, from talking and learning how to walk to putting on their clothes and handling money. Sometimes we say to them, "You better do this or you ought to do that." Perhaps what we should be saying is, "Do what God wants you to do," or, "Is that decision in keeping with His will for your life?" We should take advantage of every opportunity to transfer their sense of answerability to God instead of us parents. The most important skill we can teach our children is how to listen and follow God's direction. After all, mere man is the instrument God uses to create His intended objective of life in the flesh.

> Think of it this way. If a father dies and leaves great wealth for his young children, those children are not much better off than slaves until they grow up, even though they actually own everything their father had. They have to obey their guardians until they reach whatever age their father set. And that's the way it was with us before Christ came. We were slaves to the spiritual powers of this world. But when the right time came, God sent his Son, born of a woman, subject to the law. God sent him to buy freedom for us who were slaves to the law, so that he could adopt us as his very own children. And because you Gentiles have become his children, God has sent the Spirit of his Son into your hearts, and now you can call God your dear Father. Now you are no longer a slave but God's own child. And since you are his child, everything he has belongs to you.
>
> —GALATIANS 4:1–7

In spite of this truth, we do not give the Bible the attention it deserves, which is the key to our inheritance.

We are the role models for our children. Therefore, if God's Word is not the final authority with us, it will most likely not be the final authority for our children. The consequence is that many of our children never receive their kingdom inheritance, unless they find it on their own, because they are not taught about it. We must change this and begin to teach our children the power of the Word of God from childhood. That way, when their faith is challenged, they will be able to defend it. They will know the truth of the gospel of Jesus Christ. Knowledge of God's Word prepares us for eternal life.

Our time on Earth is temporary and short-lived and could end in a moment's notice. We need the Word of God to sustain us while we are here.

At this point I see God serving His purpose in my life in so many ways. Two years ago, I chose His way, and I already see things happening in my life that I never expected. Just the honor of being assigned this project has blessed me beyond measure. It has taken me to a level way beyond extraordinary.

> Go into all the world and preach the Good News to everyone, everywhere. Anyone who believes and is baptized will be saved. But anyone who refuses to believe will be condemned. These signs will accompany those who believe: They will cast out demons in my name, and they will speak new languages. They will be able to handle snakes with safety, and if they drink anything poisonous, it won't hurt them. They will be able to place their hands on the sick and heal them."
>
> —Mark 16:15–18

The Ultimate Weapon of Protection

I was extremely enlightened at a Christian conference I attended where a lieutenant colonel in the United States Army gave his testimony about his war experience. He was a career soldier who had served in the military for fifteen years and participated in two wars. He shared with us the story of how, during his entire ten years at war, he never lost a soldier. He recounted that, while at war, he required all the soldiers under his command to memorize Psalm 91. He wanted them to use this scripture as a tool to ensure God's hands of protection on the entire battalion daily. At the beginning of each day, the entire team recited and prayed Psalm 91. For ten years they practiced this ritual, and in that time his battalion never lost a soldier. He believed it was because it was the answer to their prayer of protection.

This lieutenant colonel's story gives us insight into how to use God's Word as a shield of protection against our enemies. Although these soldiers were equipped with earthly weapons, it was undoubtedly God's grace that shielded every one of them from death. God's shield of protection is the ultimate when we know how to use it. No soldier should be at war without the resource of the sword of God's Spirit.

I personally use Psalm 91 as my daily source of protection. It is the protection of all protection. I have memorized it so that I might use it anytime without having to refer to the Bible. I share this so that we all might be under God's protective shield:

> Those who live in the shelter of the Most High will find rest in the shadow of the Almighty. This I declare of the LORD: He alone is my refuge, my place of safety; he is my God, and I am trusting him. For he will rescue you from every trap and protect you from the fatal plague. He will shield you with his wings. He will shelter you with his feathers. His faithful promises are your armor and protection. Do not be afraid of the terrors of the night, nor fear the dangers of the day, nor dread the plague that stalks in darkness, nor the disaster that strikes at midday. Though a thousand fall at your side, though ten thousand are dying around you, these evils will not touch you. But you will see it with your eyes; you will see how the wicked are punished. If you make the LORD your refuge, if you make the Most High your shelter, no evil will conquer you; no plague will come near your dwelling. For he orders his angels to protect you wherever you go. They will hold you with their hands to keep you from striking your foot on a stone. You will trample down lions and poisonous snakes; you will crush fierce lions and serpents under your feet! The LORD says, "I will rescue those who love me. I will protect those who trust in my name. When they call on me, I will answer; I will be with them in trouble. I will rescue them and honor them. I will satisfy them with a long life and give them my salvation.
> —PSALM 91

The greatest occurrence in the Earth's realm—past, present, and going into future—is the crucifixion, burial, and resurrection of Jesus Christ and our understanding of its significance. The gospel of the good news of Jesus is intended to offer eternal salvation to all who chose to receive it. Humanity, coupled with those whom they have placed in levels of authority over nations, in their ignorance and rebellions, have abandoned the most important message ever delivered to mankind. Think about it. If mere man had the power to achieve total inner realization and complete peace without God, then why did Jesus come? God's gift of redemption to humanity by way of the cross is meaningless to both individuals and nations unless it is put to use to change the state of affairs for all people. God's truth revealed is the only source of solution for all perils. Contrarily to popular belief, our nation's leaders will in no way achieve peace and a true democratic society apart from God and in adherence to His Word.

God has purchased our freedom with his blood and has forgiven all our sins.

—Colossians 1:14

For a child is born to us, a son is given to us. And the government will rest on his shoulders. These will be his royal titles: Wonderful Counselor, Mighty God, Everlasting Father, Prince of Peace. His ever expanding, peaceful government will never end. He will rule forever with fairness and justice from the throne of his ancestor David. The passionate commitment of the Lord Almighty will guarantee this!

—Isaiah 9:6–7

May the Lord of peace himself always give you his peace no matter what happens. The Lord be with you all.

—2 Thessalonians 3:16

America in Bondage to Greed

No one ignores God and gets away with it (Isa. 22:8–13). When the Supreme Court of the United States of America removed the Ten Commandments from our schools, it was like they removed God from the position of authority. In effect the Court stole the biblical foundation of America. They also made themselves the nation's god. In essence, our nation's arbiters have given themselves the title of the Source and proclaimed themselves as the highest authority. When we remove God's standards from our world, then man is free to substitute them for his own. This happened long ago in the early days of Israel: "In those days there was no king in Israel; everyone did what was right in his own eyes" (Judg. 21:25, nkjv). The government has eliminated the higher power of what man has historically believed in, God almighty. Removing the Ten Commandments from our schools is to say, "There is no supreme law here; anything goes."

The American government has certainly ignored and defied the laws of the Creator of the universe. The subsequent wrath on our nation in events such as 9/11, the collapse of the global economy, and violence in our schools is not coincidental.

The time has come for every prophecy to be fulfilled!

—Ezekiel 12:23

Once they took the Ten Commandments from our nation, they removed God as the hedge of protection.

> For the angel of the LORD guards all who fear him, and he rescues them.
> —PSALM 34:7

It is unfortunate that our leaders are in complete ignorance to the laws of a kingdom that supersede those of the Earth's realm.

> My people are being destroyed because they don't know me.
> —HOSEA 4:6

Approximately thirty percent of the Bible concerned future events at the time it was written.

> And do not forget the things I have done throughout history. For I am God—I alone! I am God, and there is no one else like me. Only I can tell you what is going to happen even before it happens. Everything I plan will come to pass, for I do whatever I wish...Listen to me, you stubborn, evil people! For I am ready to set things right, not in the distant future, but right now! I am ready to save Jerusalem and give my glory to Israel.
> —ISAIAH 46:9–10, 12–13

America declared freedom from Great Britain in 1776, yet the nation has fallen back into bondage. Why? Basically greed and the need for instant gratification (e.g., the spend-more-than-you-have, we-must-have-it-now mentality). Greed and self-serving mentalities have intoxicated the minds of most of the leaders we have placed in positions of authority. Unfortunately, we have ignored our founding fathers. As a result, America has rejected God's headship over our nation through the leaders we placed in office and the laws we pass.

As a young nation, our leaders started with good intentions. George Washington, the nation's first president, said in his inaugural speech on April 30, 1789:

> It would be peculiarly improper to omit, in the first official Act, my fervent supplications to that Almighty Being who rules over the Universe, who presided in the Councils of Nations, and whose providential aids can supply every human defect, that his

benediction may consecrate to the liberties and happiness of the People of the United States, a Government instituted by themselves for these essential purposes.[2]

Washington also said, "No People can be bound to acknowledge and adore the invisible hand, which conducts the Affairs of men more than the People of the United States."[3]

Abraham Lincoln was a president who served God's purpose and not his own agenda. I believe he had a relationship with the Lord. The passing of the Thirteenth Amendment to abolish slavery by the Senate in April 1864, followed by the House in January 1865, was a clear depiction of Abraham Lincoln allowing the Spirit of God to work though him.

> I walk in righteousness, in paths of justice.
>
> —PROVERBS 8:20

Lincoln had a clear understanding of the judgment of God. It is so unfortunate that most leaders and politicians are lacking in their inner sense of connectedness. Lincoln managed to eradicate slavery with the passing of the Thirteenth Amendment. However, the nation has essentially reverted back to slavery and bondage without even knowing it. To have knowledge of one's status as a slave is one thing; however, to be in a place where a nation's leaders have driven people into darkness is worrisome. Whenever a society removes God from its midst it results in slavery and bondage, a place where America now finds itself.

John Adams said:

> I pray Heaven to bestow the best of blessings on this House, and all that shall hereafter inhabit it. May none but honest and wise men ever rule under this roof.[4]

> Let us hear of the dignity of [man's] nature, and the noble rank he holds among the works of God.[5]

Adams influenced the writing of the Constitution of Massachusetts of 1780. This is the beginning of Article II of that document:

> It is the right as well as the duty of all men in society, publicly and at stated seasons, to worship the Supreme Being, the great Creator and Preserver of the universe.[6]

Thomas Jefferson said:

> God who gave us life gave us liberty. Can the liberties of a nation be
> secure when we have removed a conviction that these liberties are
> the gift of God? Indeed I tremble for my country when I reflect that
> God is just, that his justice cannot sleep forever.[7]

> If we are to guard against ignorance and remain free, it is the
> responsibility of every American to be informed.[8]

> Adore God. Reverence and cherish your parents. Love your
> neighbor as yourself, and your country more than yourself. Be just.
> Be true. Murmur not at the ways of Providence.[9]

James Madison said, "The belief in a God all-powerful, wise and good,
is so essential to the moral order of the world and to the happiness of man
that arguments which enforce it cannot be drawn from too many sources
nor adapted with too much solicitude to the different characters and capac-
ities impressed with it."[10]

Benjamin Franklin is quoted at the foot of the Statue of Liberty as saying,
"They that can give up essential liberty to obtain a little safety deserve neither liberty nor safety." He also declared:

> I have lived, Sir, a long time, and the longer I live, the more con-
> vincing proofs I see of this truth—that God governs in the affairs
> of men. And if a sparrow cannot fall to the ground without His
> notice, is it probable that an empire can rise without His aid?[11]

> Freedom is not a gift bestowed upon us by other men, but a right
> that belongs to us by the laws of God and nature.[12]

> Man will ultimately be governed by God or by tyrants.[13]

Another founder, James Garfield, said:

> Now, more than ever before, the people are responsible for the
> character of their Congress. If that body be ignorant, reckless and
> corrupt, it is because the people tolerate ignorance, recklessness
> and corruption. If it be intelligent, brave and pure, it is because
> the people demand these high qualities to represent them in the
> national legislature...If the next centennial does not find us a

great nation...it will be because those who represent the enterprise, the culture, and the morality of the nation do not aid in controlling the political forces.[14]

As we can see from some of our early presidents' quotes, America began with a love and respect for God. However, as time passed God became irrelevant, and the government became the expert. The nation began to place its sights on things and not the Creator of things. Thus the country's status deteriorated. "The cares of this world and the deceitfulness of riches" (Matt. 13:22, NKJV), and the lust for other things, choked out the life of God in all. Humanity is quick to call those who are lacking intellectual or world knowledge ignorant. Likewise, those of us who lack Word-of-God wisdom are ignorant to the things that matter most, the biblical tools required for eternal life. Spiritual darkness is a result of outright rebellion to God.

If God is able to take care of the birds, why does mankind not deem Him capable?

> "Therefore I tell you, do not worry about your life, what you will eat or drink; or about your body, what you will wear. Is not life more important than food, and the body more important than clothes? Look at the birds of the air; they do not sow or reap or store away in barns, and yet your heavenly Father feeds them. Are you not much more valuable than they? Who of you by worrying can add a single hour to his life? And why do you worry about clothes? See how the lilies of the field grow. They do not labor or spin. Yet I tell you that not even Solomon in all his splendor was dressed like one of these. If that is how God clothes the grass of the field, which is here today and tomorrow is thrown into the fire, will he not much more clothe you, O you of little faith? So do not worry, saying, 'What shall we eat?' or 'What shall we drink?' or 'What shall we wear?' For the pagans run after all these things, and your heavenly Father knows that you need them. But seek first his kingdom and his righteousness, and all these things will be given to you as well. Therefore do not worry about tomorrow, for tomorrow will worry about itself. Each day has enough trouble of its own."
> —MATTHEW 6:25–34, NIV

I believe America's underlying problem is a spiritual one. It appears that most Americans, including Christians, no longer believe God judges people that rebel against Him. The Bible clearly teaches that both individuals and nations are accountable to God. I have singled out America here, because it was a nation that started out with a love for God yet lost its footing along the way. I believe that when a nation chooses to remove the hands of God from its midst it also removes His hands of protection. God cannot protect a people or a nation unless there is genuine repentance and a sincere effort to change direction from sin and outright rebellion to righteousness. True belief in the Word of God never creates a system of bondage; instead, it teaches about the true Source of all protection.

The laws of the kingdom of God are very specific, and the penalties for disobedience are extremely severe. Sometimes, the more we are given, the more we expect, want, and finally take, by any means necessary.

Do we discern His hand at work, or do we see things as mere occurrences (Isa. 8:11)? Why does the Bible deserve attention by our nation? The Bible contains God's message for humanity. America's leaders have fallen prey to the same mistakes and arrogance as Israel's first king. King Saul stopped seeking God's advice and wisdom turn to man's, and his kingdom was destroyed (1 Sam. 31).

> All Scripture is inspired by God and is useful to teach us what is true and to make us realize what is wrong in our lives. It straightens us out and teaches us to do what is right. It is God's way of preparing us in every way, fully equipped for every good thing God wants us to do.
>
> —2 TIMOTHY 3:16–17

In the grand scheme of things, the one relationship that really matters is the one with our Redeemer and Lord. I believe that a nation's genuine repentance is the key to reconciliation and the only solution to turning the tide from continued shipwreck.

It is my intention to use this book to help us all shed our sinful nature and begin the journey toward an intimate, personal relationship with our Creator. How?

- Read the Word of God.

- Listen to Holy-Spirit direction.

- Pray to develop a relationship with our Creator.

- Do the Word of God.

HOLY SPIRIT IS OUR HELPER

And the Holy Spirit helps us in our distress. For we don't even know what we should pray for, nor how we should pray. But the Holy Spirit prays for us with groanings that cannot be expressed in words. And the Father who knows all hearts knows what the Spirit is saying, for the Spirit pleads for us believers in harmony with God's own will. And we know that God causes everything to work together for the good of those who love God and are called according to his purpose for them.

ROMANS 8:26–28

WHO IS THE Holy Spirit? He is the third person of the Trinity. He is eternal and fully God. He is omnipotent. Mary asked the angel, "But how can I have a baby? I am a virgin" (Luke 1:34). The angel replied, "The Holy Spirit will come upon you, and the power of the Most High will overshadow you. So the baby born to you will be holy, and he will be called the Son of God" (Luke 1:37). Nothing is impossible with God. He is also omniscient and omnipresent.

> I can never escape from your spirit! I can never get away from your presence!
>
> —PSALM 139:7

God desires to help us and wants to be involved in every phase of our lives. For a believer, the Holy Spirit is our psychologist, therapist, spiritual consultant, and personal advisor during all our struggles. Consider this: We have an omniscient Creator who has assigned Himself as helper for those who believe in Him. Why, then, would we depend on the professional experience of mere man as our only source of help for our emotional, spiritual, and physical health? Many of these professionals neither know nor believe in God. Hence, the advice will result ineffectual if we don't have our own, personal spiritual grounding.

> Who is able to advise the Spirit of the LORD? Who knows enough to be his teacher or counselor? Has the LORD ever needed

19

anyone's advice? Does he need instruction about what is good or
what is best? No, for all the nations of the world are nothing in
comparison with him. They are but a drop in the bucket, dust on
the scales. He picks up the islands as though they had no weight at
all. All Lebanon's forests do not contain sufficient fuel to consume
a sacrifice large enough to honor him. All Lebanon's sacrificial animals would not make an offering worthy of our God. The nations
of the world are as nothing to him. In his eyes they are less than
nothing—mere emptiness and froth.

—ISAIAH 40:13–17

True wisdom only comes from God through those who are in relationship with Him. Earthly credentials, without God, leads mankind into perpetual darkness.

When Jesus was physically in the earth's realm, He asked that we believe
and follow Him. He said to His disciples—which applies to believers
today—"I will ask Father, and he will give you another Counselor" (John
14:16). That Comforter is the Holy Spirit, our Helper, who's core purpose
is to guide believers into truth (Acts 1:8). The Holy Spirit is our moral
influence and the executor of God's nature in our lives. How does the
Holy Spirit guide us? The Holy Spirit will not speak on His own authority.
Whatever He hears He will speak, and He will deliver it to the spirit of
man. This only takes place in the lives of believers who have an intimate,
personal communication with Jesus. God is bigger than any of our experiences. Jesus had the Holy Spirit without limitation, and He said we would
have more than He did.

The truth is, anyone who believes in me will do the same works I
have done, and even greater works, because I am going to be with
the Father. You can ask for anything in my name, and I will do it,
because the work of the Son brings glory to the Father. Yes, ask
anything in my name, and I will do it!

—JOHN 14:12–14

SHEKINAH GLORY

In the summer of 2009, I had a dream that God's shekinah glory would
come upon me. In the dream, God manifested His presence. However, I
was not clear of what form the manifestation would take, when it would
take place, or how it would come upon me. I did get a sense that however the manifestation revealed itself, it would be in the form of something

beyond my imagination. What was clear is that it would happen at some point during my earthly life existence. Indeed, an audible voice of the King of kings and Lord of lords is the form in which it ultimately came, and it was beyond my wildest expectations. I certainly did not expect to hear an audible voice from the Lord.

The term *shekinah glory* refers to the presence of God on Earth or a symbol of His presence manifested in our lives. It is the glory of God's radiance of His holiness, love, and power. The same week I had the dream, I attended my regular Friday evening Bible study, and low and behold, the rabbi's teaching that evening was about the shekinah glory of the Lord. I knew from my studies that it was a supernatural and extraordinary blessing. However, the lesson clarified some of my questions regarding the shekinah glory of God.

After that Friday evening I continued with my studies and did not think about it again. I was committed to study the Word of God in my every available moment, and I managed to stay focused, putting all else aside. Because many of the relational commitments I had experienced with individuals in the earthly realm left me unfulfilled, I decided to commit my all to God. God said it in the following in scripture, and I took Him at His Word:

> Obey all the laws Moses gave you. Do not turn away from them, and you will be successful in everything you do. Study this Book of the Law continually. Meditate on it day and night so you may be sure to obey all that is written in it. Only then will you succeed. I command you—be strong and courageous! Do not be afraid or discouraged. For the LORD your God is with you wherever you go.
> —JOSHUA 1:7–9

On a Saturday evening, on June 17, 2012, at exactly 6:45 p.m., God's imminent blessing came upon me. The shekinah glory of God came in an audible form. I had just returned home from having an early dinner and had planned to review one of the chapters in my manuscript. I sat in the den on the computer and started to review a particular chapter. I began reading from the computer screen, and all of a sudden I literally heard a voice reading the words from my document loud and clear. It took me a second to realize what was happening, and finally it dawned on me that it was the Lord. I was in awe. I said, "It is God! It is the Lord. It is really You."

To this day I am not sure of the true meaning of what happened. I concluded that God wanted me to know that He was pleased with my obedience to the assignment. I believe He was also pleased that I had allowed the Spirit to lead the project. After the last word, when the voice stopped, I knew it was most definitely an audible manifestation of omnipotent power of God. It was my 2009 dream of the presence of God upon me, the shekinah glory coming to fruition.

The voice of the Lord started here: Revelation from the Spirit only comes to believers through and from God. It comes when we have an intimate personal relationship with Jesus by His Spirit.

> His Spirit searches out everything and shows us God's deep secrets. No one can know what anyone else is really thinking except that person alone, and no one can know God's thoughts except God's own Spirit.
> —1 CORINTHIANS 2:10–11

Who are we? Until we find the answer to this question we will never discover our purpose on the earth. It is very unfortunate that many of us believe that self-discovery is accomplished through receiving validation from other human beings. According to the Word of God, we are made in His image and were created for a specific purpose: to accomplish the will of God. Our being should be modeled from His existence. However, because of our fallen nature, we lack the ability to know God apart from His willingness to reveal Himself. Man's logic cannot identify God. Therefore, mere man will never be able to know our Creator unless He chooses to reveal Himself.

The Spirit of God reveals His Word. When we read the Bible, we see the different ways He spoke. This is the guideline provided for all humanity. The Bible was transmitted through the power of the Holy Spirit and recorded in written format. God used human agents to document the Word. However, authors were working under the power of the Holy Spirit. To know Jesus requires a revelation from the Holy Spirit. Many profess belief in Jesus. However, true belief is only demonstrated by the Holy Spirit, which abides in the believer. The Holy Spirit is within us all.

Be aware: "The truth is, no one can enter the Kingdom of God without being born of water and the Spirit. Humans can reproduce only human life, but the Holy Spirit gives new life from heaven. So don't be surprised at my statement that you must be born again. Just as you can hear the wind but can't tell where it comes from or where it is going, so you can't explain how people are born of the Spirit" (John 3:5–8).

Unbelievers are in rebellion to God, while many Christians are in a state of complacency. This creates a real dilemma! Why? How can a fallen world come to know God? Isaiah captured it so vividly when he said:

No wonder we grope like blind people and stumble along. Even at brightest noontime, we fall down as though it were dark. No wonder we are like corpses when compared to vigorous young men!
—Isaiah 59:10

Jesus instituted a system of discipleship for believers. However, in order to accomplish this directive, believers need to adhere to the teaching and transmit it to others. To receive Holy-Spirit revelation we need to spend time in the Word. For me personally, although I had been a Christian for most of my life, revelation manifested itself only when I freed myself from religious activities and stepped into relationship with God. God had been silent with me for a very long time. I now realize that His silence was meant to bring me to a deeper understanding of His spirit within me. I never heard an audible response from Him until my experience with the shekinah glory. In His omnipotence, God demonstrates the supernaturally extraordinary in different ways. The audible voice took me into a whole new level in my relationship with Him. In the past I experienced a nudge, a sign, a vision, a dream, a message, and unwarranted favor in various forms. However, this scripture validates my audible experience with God perfectly:

Eye has not seen, nor ear heard, Nor have entered into the heart of man The things which God has prepared for those who love Him.
—1 Corinthians 2:9, nkjv

I never understood the working of the Holy Spirit until I experienced adversity and sought solace in the Word of God. The decision to pursue God is by no means an effortless one. However, it is a daily practice where our heart, thoughts, and words must align with what He says in the Bible. Ultimately, the reward supernaturally exceeds any other accomplishment one would hope to achieve in this life and in the earth's realm. An intimate relationship with God, through the Holy Spirit, allows us to become one with our Creator. God speaks in so many ways; we only get our steps when we pay attention. Directions come the same way as a GPS, one step at a time. We take the first step, and then He shows us the next.

But God speaks again, though people do not recognize it. He speaks in dreams, in visions of the night when deep falls on people as they lie in bed.
—Job 33:14–15

ALWAYS FOLLOW THE PROMPTINGS OF THE HOLY SPIRIT

There are no *ifs* in God's plans!

There is a process to receive from God:

- Hear the Word.

- Make your request known.

- Have faith in the Word.

- Meditate on the Word.

- Obey the Word.

FOLLOW THROUGH WITH CORRESPONDING ACTION FROM OUR CREATOR

When I first received the revelation for this assignment, I had no idea where to begin. The Word of God was stored in my heart and my thoughts. From my study of God's Word, I knew one thing for certain: He would provide direction. My responsibility was to pay attention. I was aware that I needed to keep my spirit in agreement and connected to His Spirit in order to receive guidance. I did it by meditating on His Word continuously. After my initial response of denial to the revelation, coupled with anxiety, I knew that my only option was to move forward in obedience. It dawned on me that God was looking for my availability, not my ability. He has all the capability.

I knew that I was in a state of brokenness created by my own ignorance to the Word of God. This was the place where it would be proven whether I was rightly selected for the job. I am forever grateful to have been in a position where I experienced a continuous series of harsh conditions, which contributed to my enlightenment. I learned from my study that when one is called by God to do something, one's present circumstances should never be used to determine one's qualifications for the assignment. Instead, one should use the Holy Spirit as his or her guide, as He will orchestrate every force possible to accomplish His will. All that is ever required is willingness and trust to take on the task, to receive, obey, believe, have faith, and act on the revelation.

God does not expect us to understand; He just wants us to trust Him and move forward with the request one step at a time. There are times when we are unclear about what has been discerned. However, whether we allow the vision to turn into character depends on us, not Him. As I study the Bible and receive enlightenment, I learn to live in reliance on what was revealed not only through the message but also the vision. I thank God daily for the clear demands He has made on my life. God has used so many different means to provide opportunities to make me useful to accomplish His will. Through my studies I now have a better understanding of some of what happens in the lives of others.

Abide in Him

Jesus showed us in Scripture how to abide. God's requirement to abide is obedience coupled with faith and trust in Him.

> When you obey me, you remain in my love, just as I obey my Father
> and remain in his love…u are my friends if you obey me.
> —John 15:10, 14

How do we abide? We stay connected to the Father, the Source of all things. True wisdom only comes from God, and when we abide, we dwell in the relationship through the Word daily. When we abide in Christ, we bear witness that God's Spirit of holiness lives within us. The revelation of God by His Spirit to ours enables, energizes, informs, and warns us. There is a direct relationship between the revelation of God in our lives and the time we spend in the Word. Know that our circumstances are ordained by God, and there is no such thing as chance when we abide. He brings us into situations that we do not understand. However, they are all purposed to accomplish His will.

What I have found most interesting is that unbelievers think that they are in control. What they don't understand is that God is in control of all their circumstances. Although He gave us all free will, He allows independence only to a certain degree. Those who abide in Him recognize His hands and realize that in the end, the objective is to accomplish His will here on Earth. We will not always like what God does or requires of us. However, it is not about us. It is about accomplishing the will of God for all of humanity. If we trust Him, Scripture assures that He makes all things work for the good of those who love Him and are called to His purpose (Rom. 8:28). When we read the Word, faith propels us to believe, and we develop trust.

Our Relationships

When we became Christians, the Holy Spirit came into our hearts, regenerated us, and abided in us. Grace provided the supernatural power within to produce the same fruit God produced in Jesus. God's ultimate focus is for us to be with Him for all eternity. Our greatest testimony would be a display of

His love, which never disappoints, falters, nor ends. To abide with the Spirit of God is His key objective for us and should ultimately be ours.

I have heard people say continuously that they are looking for a relationship that completes them. Prior to my discovery of truth, I was guilty of making the same type of uninformed statement. The truth is, the only person that is able to complete us is the Spirit of God within. No earthly person is able to complete us. One of the major reasons for despondency in mankind is looking for completeness outwardly. All the wholeness we need is within us. An awareness of the Spirit of God within is the only way to accomplish our desire for completeness. One of the major reasons why relationships fall apart is because most of us go into it overflowing with needs that we are looking for the other person to fulfill. All relationships have the potential to become joyous and effortless when the parties involved are aware of who they are in Christ. Without this awareness they never become conscious of the bigger picture, the will of God. There is not anyone on planet Earth that can satisfy the longing in our hearts completely.

In romantic love, people become disillusioned very quickly. Why? People basically deal from the flesh, rather than the spirit. The reality is, people change, feelings wear, and hearts wander outwardly very quickly. Today the objective in most relationships is not love. Instead it is people seeking prominence, security, and prosperity with focus on the bottom line on their financial statements. Money is not the evil. It is the love of it that creates evil.

> For the love of money is at the root of all kinds of evil. And some people, craving money, have wondered from the true faith and pierced themselves with many sorrows.
> —1 Timothy 6:10

> If you are wise and understand God's ways, live a life of steady goodness so that only good deeds will pour forth. And if you don't brag about the good you do, then you will be truly wise!
> —James 3:13

When we deal in the spirit rather than the flesh, our human distractions don't affect us in the same way. Give some thought to what your life would look like if you were to abide in God. Align your thoughts to those of God's Word. Release all independence to the promptings of the Holy Spirit. When we abide, we place ourselves on the receiving end. Many lack insight from the kingdom because they have neglected to read the Bible. In retrospect, I now see instances where God placed blessings in my life. However, I was so connected to the world's ungodly way of operation that I missed the call.

No one is able to yield to the supremacy of God independently. However, we can pray, and supernaturally, by grace, the Spirit of God will get us there. Once we reach that point, then what? We alter our lifestyle to align with His Word, not the other way around. We should be now at the point where we have a real distaste for sin. I must confess, I myself am still working on this, and it is a lifetime commitment. Very few Christians have a handle on the extent of this kind of loyalty to Christ.

If we think of ourselves as branches on a tree that need to maintain connected to the vine to remain in the light, it will give us a clearer picture of what we need to do. When a branch from a tree is separated from the vine, it dies. The same applies to us when we are not connected to the Spirit of God; when this happens, we are in darkness. Jesus said, "I am the true vine, and my Father is the gardener. He cuts off every branch that bears no fruit, while every branch that does bear fruit he prunes so that it will be even more fruitful" (John 15:1–2, NIV). You have already been pruned for greater fruitfulness by this message He is sending you.

> Remain in me, and I will remain in you. For a branch cannot produce fruit if it is severed from the vine, and you cannot be fruitful apart from me. Yes, I am the vine; you are the branches. Those who remain in me, and I in them, will produce much fruit. For apart from me you can do nothing. Anyone who parts from me is thrown away like a useless branch and withers. Such branches are gathered into a pile to be burned. But if you stay joined to me and my words remain in you, you may ask any request you like, and it will be granted! My true disciples produce much fruit. This brings great glory to my Father.
> —JOHN 15:4–8

WE ARE ACCOUNTABLE FOR THE LIGHT WE ARE GIVEN

Many Christians are under the misconception that when they receive salvation Jesus comes into their heart and lives continually into eternity. Unfortunately, salvation is just the start of the spiritual journey. There is also a fallacy among believers that pastors and/or teachers are responsible for all our spiritual learning, and we need do nothing but show up at church. However, we are required to read the guide on our own and develop in the Word so that we might become His disciples. We are only able to contribute to the building up of the whole at church when we have awareness of what the sum total entails.

> Therefore, go and make disciples of all the nations, baptizing them in the name of the Father and the Son and the Holy Spirit. Teach these new disciples to obey all the commands I have given you. And be sure of this: I am with you always, even to the end of the age.
> —MATTHEW 28:19–20

The omnipresence of God is united with the believer's spirit to allow them to live as Jesus did. Since God is Spirit, it is a personal experience of intimacy with the believer.

Scripture explains it like this:

> If you love me, obey my commandments. And I will ask the Father, and he will give you another Counselor, who will never leave you. He is the Holy Spirit, who leads into all truth. The world at large cannot receive him, because it isn't looking for him and doesn't recognize him. But you do, because he lives with you now and later will be in you.
> —JOHN 14:15–17

Reading and studying the Word of God are great activities to help us develop. However, for personal growth we need to do much more. We need to be doers of the Word, not only hearers.

> But be doers of the word, and not hearers only, deceiving your-selves. For if anyone is a hearer of the word and not a doer, he is like a man observing his natural face in a mirror; for he observes himself, goes away, and immediately forgets what kind of man he was. But he who looks into the perfect law of liberty and continues in it, and is not a forgetful hearer but a doer of the work, this one will be blessed in what he does.
> —JAMES 1:22–25, NKJV

Do not end your life without having discovered your true purpose. I am so grateful for the perils that led me to the light. Without the struggles of life we will never understand its purpose. If we miss this experience, we will go the grave missing God's will for our lives.

Doing Versus Being

The greatest threat to applying truths in the process of our spiritual development stems from our business. Many of us define ourselves in terms of our performance and achievements. We miss relational opportunities with our Creator when we are focused and preoccupied with valueless activities. Consider some of the activities on your priority list, like television, sports, time on the computer, social media, and many others that arguably add no value to your development. You must evaluate which activity is worth giving up to commence a relationship with your Creator.

God has a better system in place and gave us a guide to get there successfully. Our Creator wants to show us more of Him. God is interested in the time we spend in His Word so that He might show us things to come. We only get to know Him from the Word outlined in the guide He provided. Word time equates to know-how in the operation in the realm of the spirit. Many Christians are so overwhelmed with activities and works that they have no time to spend in the Word. This is a big mistake because ignorance to the Word of God results in fruitlessness in our lives.

The following is a biblical example of doing versus being:

> As Jesus and the disciples continued on their way to Jerusalem, they came to a village where a woman named Martha welcomed them into her home. Her sister, Mary, sat at the Lord's feet, listening to what he taught. But Martha was worrying over the big dinner she was preparing. She came to Jesus and said, "Lord, doesn't it seem unfair to you that my sister just sits here while I do all the work? Tell her to come and help me." But the Lord said to her, "My dear Martha, you are so upset over all these details! There is really only one thing worth being concerned about. Mary has discovered it— and I won't take it away from her."
> —Luke 10:38–42

It is time to get away from all the business that has nothing to do with God. We need to get our spiritual relationship with our Creator developed.

> The sacrifice you want is a broken spirit. A broken and repentant heart, O God, you will not despise.
> —Psalm 51:17

> But that is the time to be careful! Beware that in your plenty you
> do not forget the LORD your God and disobey his commands, reg-
> ulations, and laws.
>
> —DEUTERONOMY 8:11

There are enumerable blessings and or curses we bring upon ourselves
because of our ignorance to the Word of God. And guess what? We continuously blame God because we elected not to educate ourselves on the
laws of the kingdom.

> People ruin their lives by their own foolishness and then are angry
> at the LORD.
>
> —PROVERBS 19:3

DISOBEDIENCE RELEASES CURSES

The devil has deceived many people into thinking that they are an exception
to the Word of God. When we violate the principles of Scripture the consequences are devastating. Believers should be wise enough to look around
and see the consequences of disobedience and flee from it.

> Cursed are those who put their trust in mere humans and turn
> their hearts away from the LORD.
>
> —JEREMIAH 17:5

We all have a belief system from which we have convictions. What are your
convictions based on? If they are not based on the truth of the God's Word
we stand to increase our perils. God is sovereign. He rules over all people
and all things, and we will never understand why He allows certain things.
However, Scripture tells us that His thoughts and ways are way higher than
ours; He sees the end, while humans can only relate to the now (Isa. 55:8).

God does not make believers immune to perils. However, He provides us
with the necessary grace to see things through to a satisfactory conclusion.

OBEDIENCE RELEASES BLESSINGS

Obedience to God always brings blessings. Faith and love are the requirements that govern the kingdom of God's system. We cannot reap the benefits of His promises without having faith and love for all others. When we
purpose to follow God's will in obedience, He then becomes responsible
for the outcome in our lives. Would you want God to be responsible for the
outcomes in your life? What an awesome promise. Scripture tells us:

> Today I am giving you the choice between a blessing and a curse!
> You will be blessed if you obey the commands of the LORD your
> God that I am giving you today. You will receive a curse if you
> reject the commands of the LORD your God and turn from his way
> by worshiping foreign gods.
> —DEUTERONOMY 11:26–28

As Christians, we are a part of the kingdom of God and are free to choose either obedience or disobedience, knowing that one will produce blessings and the other curses. Where are you today in your journey? Have you chosen to obey God? God promises to love us unconditionally. However, it is our obedience that activates the blessing in our lives.

Divine discernment of this book came from obedience and adherence to the Word. Although obedience leads to blessings, it does not just show up. It requires spending a great deal of time the Word. This has been the most challenging and, at the same time, most rewarding experience in my entire life. I am truly living in the light of God and for the first time free from the oppression of the world. This journey requires Word-of-God commitment, coupled with meditation to tap into the Holy Spirit, the real Teacher. The Spirit Helper provides understanding and counsel in the steps to align God's commands and listen for the wise course of action to take.

If we are to ever climb to the heights of the supernaturally extraordinary in God's revelation, later is not an option; it must be now. Let's look at the testing of Abraham's faith as it relates to his obedience. The Lord spoke to Abraham and said:

> Take your son, your only son—yes, Isaac whom you love so much—
> and go to the land of Moriah. Sacrifice him there as a burnt offering
> on one of the mountains, which I will point out to you. The next
> morning Abraham got up early. He saddled his donkey and took two
> of his servants with him, along with his son Isaac. Then he chopped
> wood to build a fire for a burnt offering and set out for the place where
> God had told him to go. On the third day of the journey, Abraham
> saw the place in the distance. "Stay here with the donkey," Abraham
> told the young men. "The boy and I will travel a little farther. We will
> worship there, and then we will come right back." Abraham placed
> the wood for the burnt offering on Isaac's shoulders, while he himself
> carried the knife and fire. As the two of them went on together, Isaac
> said, "Father?" "Yes, my son," Abraham replied. "We have the wood
> and the fire," said the boy, "but where is the lamb for the sacrifice?"

"God will provide a lamb, my son," Abraham answered. And they
both went on together. When they arrived at the place where God
had told Abraham to go, he built an altar and placed the wood on it.
Then he tied Isaac up and laid him on the altar over the wood. And
Abraham took the knife and lifted it up to kill his son as a sacrifice to the LORD. At that moment, the angel of the LORD shouted to
him from heaven, "Abraham! Abraham!" "Yes" he answered. "I'm listening." "Lay down the knife," the angel said. "Do not hurt the boy in
any way, for now I know that you truly fear God. You have not with-
held even your beloved son from me." Abraham then looked and saw
a ram caught by its horns in a bush. So he took the ram and sacrificed
it as a burnt offering on the altar in place of his son. Abraham named
the place "The LORD Will Provide." This name has now become a
proverb: "On the mountain of the LORD it will be provided."
                                             —GENESIS 22:2–14

They are so many things clamoring for attention that as believers it is
very difficult to discern directions that are coming from the Holy Spirit.
It takes a great deal of time in God's Word to develop intimacy with His
Spirit within us. Therefore, speak less, listen more, and pay attention to the
inner Spirit's counsel. Trust in God only comes with faith that His Word
will do what it says.

Abraham did not delay in the task he was given because his trust in God
was greater than the fear of losing his beloved son. He knew that God's
power would bring his son back to life. Would you trust God with your
most beloved? Trust in God is not conceivable without the relationship. If
you have no relationship with a person, it is impossible to trust them. The
same applies to the relationship with Creator of the universe. It behooves
all of us to gain guidance and wisdom from the Book.

Flesh gives birth to flesh, but the Spirit gives birth to spirit.
                                             —JOHN 3:6, NIV

3

GOD PROMISES TO BE THE SOURCE FOR ALL OUR NEEDS

I N ORDER TO make God the Source, as He promised to be, it is crucial that we place ourselves in a position of allowance. The free will that God provided to all of humanity does not allow Him to be our Source without our permission.

Therefore, we must open ourselves up, let go, and allow Him to become our Source. God made a covenant with us and will not break it. We have an awesome defense force, and when we make God our Source, nothing can defeat us unless it is His will and He has a reason for it. There is absolutely no need that our Source is not able to provide.

> Don't put your confidence in powerful people; there is no help for you there. When their breathing stops, they return to the earth, and in a moment all their plans come to an end. But happy are those who have the God of Israel as their helper, whose hope is in the LORD their God. He is the one who made the heaven and earth, the sea, and everything in them. He is the one who keeps every promise forever, who gives justice to the oppressed and food to the hungry. The LORD frees the prisoners.
> —PSALM 146:3–7

However, God cannot and will not become our Source on the basis of our criteria. It has to be based on our commitment and obedience to His Word. Instead of talking about our problems, we must develop a relationship with the only Source that is able to resolve every crisis. We cannot expect for God to be our puppet to fix things in our lives whenever we say so. The only way to make God our source is to give him first place in every area of our lives.

> It is the Spirit who gives eternal life. Human effort accomplishes nothing. And the very words I have spoken to you are spirit and life.
> —JOHN 6:63

We must let go and allow God to be our source. When we don't, perils prevail. I have a friend from a past relationship who has suffered a total of three strokes within the span of about five years. Although he is a believer, he spent his entire life in a self-serving mode. Now, as a result of his physical condition, he is angry at the Lord. He was advised to repent of his wrongdoings and meditate on God's Word. However, his angry state of mind toward the Lord would not open His heart to repent. Now he considers himself the victim and believes it is God's fault that he is in the state he is in. If he ever would take the time to receive the revelation of who he is in Christ, he would realize that God is in control of all things. Instead of playing the victim, he should use the opportunity to develop spiritually and become a victor. Salvation for this individual might have been an action to ensure the security of gaining access into the kingdom. However, after salvation, he did not consider that there was a second, third, and possibly fourth step he needed to take. He was having too much fun following the wicked ways of the world. As a believer, God provided him with the tool of His uncompromising Word to live a life of heaven in the Earth's realm. However, because of his unwillingness to develop in the truth of God's Word, he is now suffering the consequences of his behavior.

Many believers are suffering the same way with all sorts of maladies due to similar behavior. Imagine suffering that many strokes and still not receiving the message that God wants your attention. God certainly was not the cause of the stroke; however, He allowed it. What has happened to my friend is a scenario in which many people find themselves. They know of a Creator, but they have no relationship with Him. When things go wrong they get angry with the Lord. Would you expect a person who you knew but had no relationship with to resolve your problems? I believe not. I would imagine you would get started by getting to know the person.

I believe the reason many believers find themselves in the position of suffering is that they never committed to making God their Source. When sickness comes upon their body, instead of consulting with their Maker, they run to the doctors and commence with medication. There is nothing wrong with going to a physician, but that should never be the sole choice. A conversation with God needs to be the first step. If we want God to be our Source, then He needs to be consulted before we look to other sources.

The death of Jesus was not something that just happened that could have been avoided or prevented. It was the reason for His coming and is the final word in the redemption of humankind. At the cross, Jesus confronted the sin that humanity received from Adam. Until the presentation of this message is clear, we will continue not to see our Creator as our Source.

> For God made Christ, who never sinned, to be the offering for our
> sin, so that we could be made right with God through Christ.
> —2 Corinthians 5:21

Throughout Scripture God promises the faithful that He would provide for them. In story after story He has demonstrated His extraordinary ability to satisfy physical, emotional, and, financial needs of all His creation. Scripture states, "My God will meet all your needs according to his glorious riches in Christ Jesus" (Phil. 4:19, NIV). Jesus told His disciples not to worry about food or clothing. Since the Father watches over even the birds in the air, we can certainly count on Him to be our Source (Matt. 6:25–26).

Where do you go for solutions? God is our Source for all needs. He made all things and is supreme over all. When God created the universe, in His omniscience, He anticipated the needs of Earth's population and provided the Book as the resource to guide and direct our every step for living in Earth's realm. When we have a revelation of God as the true and only Source and then step out in faith with confidence, we can know that He will lead the way.

Sometimes Christians come into the family of the kingdom of God under the assumption that the Lord will devote Himself to our eternal happiness and we will never experience perils. This is a complete fallacy. Although God is our Source, He satisfies needs based on His will for mankind. The story of the Apostle Paul illustrates this well. Paul was used greatly by God; however, his life was far from easy. He endured unimaginable perils. But one thing was for sure: he knew his Source. When he and Silas were whipped, placed in custody, and locked in a dungeon, instead of complaining they sang hymns and praised God! What was the outcome? Suddenly there was a violent earthquake, the foundation of the prison was shaken, and immediately all the prison doors flew open. The chains of all the prisoners were loosened. The jailer, terrified, fell to Paul's feet and asked, "What must I do to be saved?" Paul then led the man and his entire household to salvation (Acts 16).

Believers must know that we will all experience perils. There is no such thing as a life without suffering, and it is most acceptable to ask God to relieve us from it. However, keep in mind, the answer may not come the way we like, as He might see deficiencies and complications that we are unaware of. Under such circumstances, we should endure and trust Him for the outcome. We can never complain our way out of a problem. Paul trusted God and was able to endure one peril after another and always remained in thanksgiving. When we have an intimate, personal relationship with the Lord, we know and can trust His Word that "God causes everything to work together for the good of those who love God and are called according to his purpose for them" (Rom. 8:28). The Apostle Paul had a great revelation of his true Source.

Most in levels of authority over others, in many spectrums of business and government, have yet to figure out their true role for service. This shortcoming makes leading arduous. Why is this? God is not at the center of anything. Hence, man will continue to make bad decisions and, at times, no decision at all. It does not matter how many PhDs or other degrees we have earned in a lifetime. Without awareness of the true Source and ignorance of the laws of the kingdom of God, the focus of world leaders becomes one of self-serving agendas rather than designed objectives to serve the populations who appointed them. It is unfortunate that we are living in a world where the majority of authority figures are the main abusers of systems.

We cannot blame God for the state of the world. He has not punished us or created our perils; we have done it to ourselves. When we are engaged in the Word of God, what is occurring in the world today should be of no surprise. Scripture is being fulfilled. All of the bad seeds that have been planted throughout the Earth, personally or by those in levels of authority, are retuning as a harvest exactly as planted, good or bad. Unfortunately for us, the seeds planted by the world system are overwhelmingly harvesting negatively. We are now experiencing the fruits of the world system of darkness. Under the kingdom law we reap what we sow later and greater.

> Nothing in all creation can hide from him. Everything is naked and exposed before his eyes. This is the God to whom we must explain all that we have done.
> —HEBREWS 4:13

> Don't be like them, because your Father knows exactly what you need even before you ask him!
> —MATTHEW 6:8

THE SOURCE IN OPERATION

On the arrival of the disciples to Capernaum, the tax collector for the Temple tax asked Peter "Doesn't your teacher pay the Temple tax? "Of course he does," Peter replied. Then he went into the house to talk to Jesus about it. But before he had a chance to speak, Jesus asked him, "What do you think, Peter? Do kings tax their own people or the foreigners they have conquered?" "They tax the foreigners," Peter replied. "Well, then," Jesus said, "the citizens are free! However, we don't want to offend them, so go down to the lake and throw in a line. Open the mouth of the first fish you catch, and you will find a coin. Take the coin and pay the tax for both of us."

—MATTHEW 17:24–27

God is the Source in and over all. Be open and receive guidance and revelation when you apply the principles in His Word. We were given access to the book of wisdom and given a choice concerning its usage. When you receive direction, do not question God. Just obey.

WISDOM FROM ABOVE

If we lack knowledge of the wisdom from above and have no expectation of supernatural intervention during times of need, there is no way we can prepare for or endure the perils of life. Throughout my seven years of unemployment, the only thing that kept me standing was my knowledge of the Word. Before I met Jesus and developed an, intimate personal relationship with Him, I clamored to find peace in a world overwhelmed in bondage and darkness. This experience would not have been possible to endure without receiving His revelation that the Creator of our universe is our true and only Source.

We cannot rely on our employer or the government as our source for survival. These worldly benefits can be taken away from us at any time. Although I was great at saving and not overwhelmed with credit card debt, my experience with unemployment brought me to a whole new level in humbleness and understanding of the plight of others. I knew I had enough savings to last for at least two years, but my joblessness lasted for much longer than that. This experience, in retrospect, shaped my character. Were it not for my knowledge of the Word of God and faith in His acts, I would not have made it through. God truly provided for me during that time.

As we learn more about God, we are able to trust and elevate Him to Lord over our lives and recognize Him as ruler over all the earth. The same friendship He offered the original twelve disciples, He offers us today. We have been privileged to be a part of this extraordinary faith journey because we know that He laid down His life for us out of love and devotion. God has made us privy to all. There are no secrets to His kingdom. We have the Book with all the steps to live successfully according to the kingdom, not world, standard. This is what Jesus said: "I no longer call you servants, because a master doesn't confide in his servants. Now you are my friends, since I have told you everything the Father told me" (John 15:15).

As I was reading the Bible one day, I discovered a scripture in Joshua that spoke to my spirit; I then adopted its principles and practiced it daily. It said, "Study this Book of the Law continually. Meditate on it day and night so you may be sure to obey all that is written in it. Only then will you succeed. I command you—be strong and courageous! Do not be afraid or discouraged. For the LORD your God is with you wherever you go" (Josh. 1:8–9). This is the scripture that kept me anchored in belief in my Source. I took this to heart and have been mindful to adhere. Our Father in heaven has given us authority to take His Word and believe that He will do what it says. This was and still is an anchor scripture for me; it is in my thoughts and heart daily.

God is the Source of every blessing. However, when we cherish the blessings more than our relationship with the One who provided the blessing, we might find ourselves stripped away from some of the benefits. I heard a testimony at a conference in which the person shared that they prayed for a beach home and received it. However, once they got the home, they pretty much ignored God. They stopped praying, going to church, and tithing. Instead, all their time was spent at work and, on the weekends, at the beach house. A couple of years later, there were cutbacks at their place of employment, and they were let go. The experience was devastating. However, it did not take them long to figure what happened. They were no longer praying; hence, they were declaring, "I am my own source. I no longer need God," and lost His protective shield. After they were blessed, they ignored the Source. Instead, they allowed the beach house to become their god.

When we turn from obedience for even a minute, darkness immediately shows its ugly face. Once we repent and get back in obedience, light returns at once. Immerse in truth and allow it to work in you.

The Bible is truly the resource to help us make honorable choices. When we obey, we allow God to be responsible for the outcome. As I reflect back on my experiences, had I known God in the intimate light in which I now know Him, I would have involved Him in my life immediately. Perhaps it would have shortened the duration of my perils. When we experience perils in our lives, it is always difficult and painful. However, the knowledge and development we gain from them supersedes the pain we endure. I would not change my experience if I could, because the wisdom I received from it far exceeds anything I could imagine. I am no longer in a state of ignorance as I once was and as many others in the body of Christ still are. The experience allowed me to get my priorities in order. God now has my undivided attention. I often think of a quote by Helen Keller: "When one door of happiness closes, another opens; but often we look so long at the closed door that we do not see the one which has been opened for us."[1] When I look back, I realize that I wasted so much unnecessary time analyzing the closed door. I have now learned to surrender to the Master and follow Holy Spirit direction. By not taking the time to get to know God, you may be missing the most meaningful relationship of your life. No other relationship will ever be greater, including the one with your children or significant other.

LEARN THE WAYS OF YOUR SOURCE

God's top priority is for us to get to know Him and become acquainted with His ways. This pursuit will continue into eternity. Every day I learn something new about our Lord. It is a fascinating journey. My relationship with Him is an extremely exciting one, always in anticipation of what He will reveal to me next. Since the relationship and understanding begins with His Word, that should be the commencement of the learning.

Initially after losing my job, I was overwhelmed with concerns and worry over my new lot in life. Little did I know that I was about to enter into the realm of the extraordinary, in the light and love of the Creator of the universe. God certainly kept his covenant promise to me. As painful as the experience was—and at times continues to be—I was delivered from a state of ignorance and bondage into the light, His light. There is a scripture in the Bible that speaks to how things are made right for those who love God and are called to His purpose, and I have seen this revealed in my life. I have seen firsthand how He makes everything right for the good of those who love Him and are called to His purpose (Rom. 8:28).

How do we learn to lean on our Source? Unfortunately, many of us don't learn until we experience perils. Scripture tells us, "Give your burdens to the LORD, and he will take care of you. He will not permit the godly to slip and fall" (Ps. 55:22). We grow in life by stumbling and faltering. We will never understand God as the true and only Source until we experience distress, difficulties, hardship, and pain. Why is this? Most only consider God when things are going badly. After the perils I experienced, I have learned that He is the fixer of all things, even those we create out of ignorance or disobedience. God's hand was in my unemployment peril, and I appreciated every step of the discipline, as well as the healing that followed.

SHAPING TOOLS

God's grace is demonstrated by the fact that He never leaves us in the same condition as we were when we come to faith. He provides tools to keep us on the track, namely:

- Prayer: To continuously keep the dialogue in the relationship with Him strong.

- A guide Book: To develop in the Christian life by reading and study of His Word.

- Church: God uses the body of believers to help in the transformation.

God has given us free will. As part of that freedom, He allows our foolish choices and, at times, He requires disciplinary action as part of our development. This action may result to be very painful. However, if taken in the right spirit in which it was intended, it will ultimately result in one of life's greatest blessings. The intent is that He might shape us into the likeness of His Son to later give Him the glory.

When we discover that this journey is not about us but about what needs to happen to accomplish God's will for mankind, we will adjust our objectives to accommodate the bigger picture.

> The LORD has made the heavens his throne; from there he rules over everything.
> —PSALM 103:19

When we believe that we are in complete control of all things, we will never get the true intent of perils. What are some of the ways we create perils? There is a scripture that speaks specifically to the role arrogance or self-centeredness plays before God steps in and makes His will known: "Pride goes before destruction, and haughtiness before a fall"(Prov. 16:18).

All of the questions you will ever experience during perils are answered when we read the Bible. The key is humbling down to God.

Have you ever surrendered a concern to God? Do you take it back later because of the need to control and fix things independently? In reality, only God has the power and perspective to bring matters to the right conclusion. When we fix things ourselves, we mostly serve our own egos. But when God gets involved, it is to the benefit of all.

For every child of God defeats this evil world by trusting Christ to give the victory.

—1 JOHN 5:4

IN SEARCH OF WHOLENESS

I knew that I was presented with a Goliath when I lost my job. However, I also recognized that I was truly blessed and one step ahead of the average person, because I had an intimate relationship with God. My greatest revelation of all was when I discovered that I did not have to face this journey in my own strength. I had the Source, the power over all, the Creator of the entire universe, on my side.

Biblical stories were one of the tools I used to develop my faith. These stories provided insight as to how God operated in the past. Since He does not change, it helped me to develop a relationship with Him.

Joseph's life was one of those stories that opened my eyes to God's use of adversity get people's attention and to accomplish His will for humanity in the earth's realm. (See Genesis 39–42.) Joseph experienced many perils in his life; however, he never allowed them to get the best of him. Instead, they were used as stepping stones to learn, develop, and endure. My objective was to learn from Joseph's experiences and use the many ways in which he responded to the difficulties presented to him as lessons on how to deal with my own situation.

Joseph was the son of Jacob and the grandson of Isaac. God had a plan for Joseph, as He does for all of us (Gen. 12). In order to be open to receive His plan for us we need to learn the ways of our Creator. In the case of Joseph, his plan was revealed in the form of dreams and visions. At this time in his life, Joseph had dreams without an understanding of their meaning and timing. One day Joseph decided to share them with his father and brothers, but it created a rift between his siblings. He was favored by his father, and this created a division among his brothers.

His wicked brothers attempted to kill him because of their jealousy, but they did not succeed. Instead, they sold him into slavery to traders, and Joseph ultimately ended up at work in the house of Potiphar, who was the chief steward of the pharaoh of Egypt. While Joseph was at Potiphar's house, his wife tried to seduce him. When he refused her advances, she accused him of rape, and he was incarcerated.

Joseph excelled during every form of adversity with which he was confronted, including the time he spent in prison. He never allowed his circumstances to get the best of him.

By now, Joseph had developed a gift for interpreting dreams. One day Pharaoh's baker and butler were being investigated and ended up in the same prison as Joseph. Both baker and butler had dreams and were told about Joseph abilities to interpret them. He was summoned to their cell, and he was able to interpret both dreams with precision. Years later, after the butler had been released from prison, Pharaoh had a dream, and his butler shared his experience with Joseph regarding dream interpretation. Joseph was summoned to appear to Pharaoh, and he listened to the dream and was able to interpret it with precision. Pharaoh recognized Joseph's resourcefulness and assigned him the job of prime minister of Egypt.

God, at times, can use the evil ones to accomplish his will for humanity. God used this entire experience of Joseph as one of learning and development. We may not understand God's ways; however, they are always meant for the greater good. God sees our future. He not only knows what's best, but He planned it all. Ultimately this position led Joseph to be the second most powerful man in Egypt, second only to Pharaoh. God would have never accomplished this through Joseph, had Joseph not responded correctly. God is Spirit; hence, we are His tools to accomplish His will in the Earth's realm.

Ultimately, there was a famine in the land of Canaan, and Joseph was able to provide for his father, Jacob, and the entire generation in Egypt. Sometimes struggles are God's way to develop not only our character but our commitment to His will. Had Joseph not learned about the God of his father, the God of Abraham, Isaac, and Jacob, he would have spent approximately thirteen years of his life succumbed by grief. These lessons were intended for humanity today.

Once you have a relationship with God, every decision you make should be based on the question, What would God have me do? We are only able to get to this point in faith when we develop the relationship with our Creator. How do we do this?

+ Come to the realization that struggles are inevitable.

+ Use the guide Book He gave us as our tool.

+ Understand that our Creator knows the beginning, middle, and end. He has the solution.

+ Trust that these instructions will work when applied to your situation.

Sowing to the Spirit

It is worth sharing a story about a job interview experience I had, which I believe was divinely directed. Several years ago I was interviewing for a position with an IT company for a business consulting opportunity. When I completed the interview and was about to leave, there was another candidate waiting in the lobby to be interviewed. As the interviewer walked me to the lobby and called the person waiting, we caught each other's eye. What happened next could only come through the light of God. The interviewer introduced us, and we immediately hugged each other. The interviewer asked us if we knew one other, and we both said no. He thought it strange that we hugged and asked, "So what is this?" The woman responded, "The light of God."

When you are in the light of God, it is easy to recognize others who are also in the light. It is almost as if we all have signs on our foreheads.

The woman then asked the interviewer how much time he required. He said forty-five minutes, and she asked me to wait if I had the time. I waited, and after her interview concluded we went to a nearby coffee shop and spent the next four hours talking about the awesomeness of God over tea. A week later we both received offers, and we both accepted. However, both our jobs ended six months later, as the company outsourced the business unit out of the country.

That experience was five years ago, and to this date we have a very strong relationship in the light of God. We both discovered that our meeting was not coincidental. We were destined to meet. Since then we have worked on a couple of initiatives together.

I have had so many experiences like this in the past seven years, where I landed a position, only to have the position eliminated in less than a year. I had a total of seven short-term projects in seven years, none lasting more than five months. But I was always able to survive against the odds. An opportunity always showed up when funds were low. One day when I opened my mail box, there was unexpectedly an envelope from my daughter. When I opened it up, there was a check for ten thousand dollars. I called her immediately, and she indicated that she was concerned about my extended period without a job and wanted to bless me. For this reason, I know for sure my Source is in control, and there is never a need to be overwhelmed or worried.

God uses many avenues to bless us. However, know that He is the ultimate Source behind every blessing. Our job or occupation may be the primary avenue; however, be clear, it is not the source. I am committed to the principal of the tithe and do so from every blessing received.

About a week after I received the check from my daughter, she talked about an idea that she had regarding tithing. She indicated that instead of giving her tithe to her church, she should give it to me since I was such a strong spiritual influence in her life. The thought was very touching. However, I knew in my heart that it was not the right thing to do. I knew that obedience was crucial, and this would be going against the Word. God said in His Word.

> "Bring all the tithes into the storehouse so there will be enough food in my Temple. If you do," says the LORD Almighty, "I will open the windows of heaven for you. I will pour out a blessing so great you won't have enough room to take it in! Try it! Let me prove it to you!"
> —MALACHI 3:10

I was not His storehouse. Therefore, to accept that suggestion would open the door to darkness in the place where I needed a huge blessing. Had I not known the biblical principles concerning tithing, I would have accepted the offer, received the money, and fallen into disobedience. I am my daughter's role model, and my ultimate objective for her is that she see how God is working in my life and use the lesson as an anchor in her own life. Trust God, and disregard how bad things might look. Never doubt that God is your true Source.

A message for the unemployed: God is your Source, not the "establishment." Make Him the center of your life, and the Holy Spirit will lead you to an opportunity. For believers who are doers of God's Word, nothing is coincidental. Do not despair. The perils we experience in life help to develop our character. Never be too proud to take a job at a lower level than what you have been accustomed to. Serve and treat it as working for God. Had I not invested the time in the Word, I would not be developed in the thing that matters most, the eternal.

There is no excuse to live in bondage and ignorance when God has given us a Book with instructions that work. Many Christians are missing the most important part of the call. The problem is that many in the body of Christ only attend church once a week and do nothing else. The belief among most is that it is the pastor's and teacher's responsibility to study and share in a sermon on Sunday.

Ways of the Flesh

I remember a time being in corporate America when Jesus was not the Lord of my life. It was interesting to spend some time back in corporate America under different circumstances. This time my main objective was doing the work with no expectations of advancement or trying to obtain a certain title. I had no interest in all the political hogwash. This time I was on assignment for the kingdom and God, with the Almighty, my Source, leading my every step. It provided a new light concerning the people and the atmosphere. I have now realized that a large percentage of the natural world, including those in the top tiers of management, is in complete darkness and bondage because they are in a state of oblivion and utter ignorance concerning their true Source.

For the most part, there continues to be a great deal of disingenuous behavior at all levels, coupled with much cluelessness regarding the true meaning of success. One of my most notable observations is how the top-tier executives in many organizations do not acknowledge those they deem as "the little people." These are the people who work and keep the company running. How ignorant not to honor and develop those relationships. I was under the impression that leaders are supposed to lead by example. This is a common attitude, though certainly not role-model behavior. The only reason any of these leaders are in these positions is by the grace of God. I challenge all of you to become the leaders that the Creator of the universe intended you to become. The Word tells us, "There is a path before each person that seems right, but it ends in death" (Prov. 16:25). How much respect can employees have for the leaders of an organization when they act like gods? Are you leading with integrity?

I have learned to disregard salary levels, titles, and other earthly accomplishments, because, in the end, they are all meaningless. As an observer with no desire of accolades from the establishment, the things I once believed to be meaningful have now lost their zeal. Once you discover your true Source, it becomes impossible to continue in the ignorance of the world system of darkness. Now that I have discovered the true Source, I sometimes feel saddened for those walking around with big egos because of the emphasis they attach to their titles, salaries, etc. Why? When a disaster strikes, they are not going to be armed with the power of God's Word. I am extremely fortunate that my perils opened the door for me to discover what remains hidden from most, the glory of God in His Word.

The most valuable lesson I learned through this experience is always to trust in God. No matter how bad things get, never lose faith, because the Word of God will do what it says. The covenant promises in the Bible only belong to believers, those who have received Jesus as Lord and Savior. Unfortunately, for those who reject God, they will continue in ignorance until perhaps some adversity or the final judgment makes them humble down.

> At the name of Jesus every knee should bow…and every tongue will confess that Jesus Christ is Lord, to the Glory of God the Father.
> —PHILIPPIANS 2:10–11

COMMITMENT TO OUR SOURCE LEADS TO BLESSINGS

I consistently seek God to lead my steps in every area of my life. In 2008, I received a clear revelation that I was to go on a trip to Israel. Actually, I had the revelation the year before, but I ignored it because of the peril of unemployment I was experiencing at the time. In my mind, I thought there was no way I could come up with the money to make the trip. In hindsight, I should have gone, because when God asks you to do something, He provides a way. I do not recommend that anyone ignore a revelation or command from the Lord. It is very big mistake, and the Spirit will continue to haunt you until you obey.

So, this time, I made plans to go. My itinerary was perfect. I was to be leaving on a direct flight from an airport near my home, and all was set. Much to my dismay, I received a letter from the travel agent stating that my flight was changed to depart from another airport nearly two hours from my home. I immediate brought my concern to God. I said, "God, I do not understand why this flight is leaving from another airport. The airport from my original itinerary is within twenty-five miles of my home, and it is going to be tremendous time and expense for me to travel to this other airport." I prayed, "God, please change the flight back to the original airport, in Jesus' name!" I then left it alone. About a month later I received a call from the travel agent indicating that the flight would be departing from the original airport. That was the grace of God!

The other issue that I asked God to fix was a roommate situation. In order to reduce expenses, I was scheduled to have a roommate on the trip, but I was not particularly keen on the idea, because I knew that since it was a spiritual trip I would want to meditate and pray on my own about the daily activities. I also was not very excited to room with a stranger on such a personal journey. Again, I prayed. I said, "God, I believe You are sending me to the Holy Land so that you might continue to develop my walk. Therefore, I am asking You to provide me with solo hotel accommodation, so that I might meditate after daily Bible studies, in Jesus' name." I then left it alone. Three days before departing, the travel agent left me a message that said, "Please call me before heading to the airport on Tuesday. I have some changes that I need to go over with you." I called that afternoon, and she said, "I have good and bad news. Which would you like first?" My response was, "Give me the bad first." She said, "You are not going to have a roommate because the person you were scheduled to room with has made some changes." I said, "Yes, Lord!" The good news was that I was not going to have to pay the additional two thousand dollars it would have cost for me to have my own room. God answered both requests!

On the fifth day of the trip a lady came up to me and said, "I heard you are the only person without a roommate." She proceeded to tell me that it was because of her. She said, "I was scheduled to be your roommate, but I wanted my husband to go. He said no, and I prayed, and four days before the trip he said he would go with me." She said, "What an awesome God we serve! He answered both our prayers, and by the way, my husband wants to reimburse you the additional two thousand dollars you paid because of my cancellation." I responded, "Guess what? It did not cost me a penny more." God says, "Listen to me! You can pray for anything, and if you believe, you will have it" (Mark 11:24). I challenge you to take God at His word.

God answers every prayer when we pray in accordance with His will, meaning the Word. He reminds us in His Word that He makes everything right for those who love Him and are called to His purpose (Rom. 8:28). God placed me among forty-four Bible-believing Christians who knew His Word and shared the same passion that I did. I received blessing after blessing on that trip. I reaffirmed my life in Christ with baptism in the Jordan River and had the opportunity to share it with people who knew God. For the first time in my life, I was able to share miracles with other Christians without being looked at as some weird alien from outer space. Many of the Christians I know seem to still be on baby formula, stuck on the fundamentals. I find myself not saying much because they think I am too radical. The believers on this trip were different. It was one of the most enlightening and uplifting experiences of my life.

There is no other source on the earth that can top the extraordinariness of God. When we are in a mode of surrender, God is able to get our attention and is able to provide clear direction. Most people have head, not heart, knowledge about God. He is the Source for not just one thing, but for everything. He is Savior, Healer, Deliverer, and much more. Open the eyes of your heart, receive this revelation, and change your life. God is the Supplier and Helper in every circumstance and all situations. The only person who knows our needs is God, and He is the only One waiting to be able to accommodate them. When we choose another Source to satisfy a need without knowing the outcome, we get into trouble. When we are in a mode of surrender, God is able to get our attention and is able to provide clear direction. Had I not discovered that I had a source in the Creator of the universe, I would have spent the last seven years in a pity party.

Good things always come from perils when you have a personal, intimate relationship with your Source. Believers, it is much later than you think! Get on board with the Book to provide you with life direction before it is too late.

THE NUMBER ONE RESOURCE TO CONQUER PERILS

The thief's purpose is to steal and kill and destroy.
My purpose is to give life in all its fullness.

JOHN 10:10

SHEDDING OUR SINFUL NATURE

SALVATION IS A gift given to all of humanity as an act of grace by the Creator of the universe. There is no other source in the Earth's realm with the power to release the world's population from sin.

> He personally carried our sins in his body on the cross so that we can be dead to sin and live for what is right. You have been healed by his wounds!
>
> —1 PETER 2:24

> He died for our sins, just as God our Father planned, in order to rescue us from this evil world in which we live.
>
> —GALATIANS 1:4

> But when people keep on sinning, it shows that they belong to the Devil, who has been sinning since the beginning. But the Son of God came to destroy the works of the Devil.
>
> —1 JOHN 3:8

When we come into the world, we are not taught about the reality of our sinful nature. Therefore, we view life through the eyes of reason. We evaluate good and bad based on the standards established by the laws of mere man. We believe that if we educate ourselves, associate with the right people, and accumulate the desired amount of money we can produce the life desired. However, we never take in to account sin and the fallen nature from which we all come. Hence, we never discover true peace. Why? Sin is a deliberate rebellion against God and is in direct conflict with love. God is love, and in Him there is absolutely no darkness.

49

It is not possible for us to have sin and God at the same time, as light and dark contrast with one another.

How do we get rid of sin? Unfortunately, we do not have the power to eliminate sin in our own strength. Only by the grace of God and in His strength are we able to rid ourselves of this demonic bondage. Acceptance of Jesus as Lord is the tool required to put this to bed. When life gets out of control, how can we maintain our peace? The key to continued peace is to follow direction from the Spirit of God within. We are only able to maintain peace tranquility and strength to overcome life's struggles when we focus on our Creator.

The voice of wisdom tells us:

> Dear brothers and sisters, whenever trouble comes your way, let it be an opportunity for joy. For when your faith is tested, your endurance has a chance to grow. So let it grow, for when your endurance is fully developed, you will be strong in character and ready for anything.
>
> —JAMES 1:2–4

APPLY GOD'S WORD TO YOUR PERILS

I embarked on a ten-year study of the Word of the living God in search of solutions to the perils I was experiencing in my life. In the process discovered truth, peace, and the joy of the Lord. I know that I cannot give anyone what I discovered. However, I pray that I might cause some to seek God and find the plan that He has prepared them.

It is my intention to use this book to help us all shed our sinful nature and begin the journey toward an intimate, personal relationship with our Creator. How?

+ Read the Word of God.

+ Listen to Holy-Spirit direction.

+ Pray to develop a relationship with our Creator.

> But the people's minds were hardened, and to this day whenever the old covenant is being read, a veil covers their minds so they cannot understand the truth. And this veil can be removed only by believing in Christ.
>
> —2 CORINTHIANS 3:14

Only when the truth of God comes to our forefront do we realize that we are all a part of a very dysfunctional society. By dysfunctional, I mean we are followers of the world system. We have diverted from God and succumbed to the world's evil ways, giving into our flesh rather than operating from our spirit. We consider dysfunctional nations, families, or persons to be those who are behaving outside of social norms. We believe we are behaving within the norm because our society has led us to that conclusion. But who sets those norms? Dysfunctional societies, for the most part, are created by the ungodly individuals we have placed in positions and levels of authority.

Our Creator is concerned about our complacency, as a people, nation, individual and family. Proverbs 1:22 (NKJV) says, "How long, you simple ones, will you love simplicity? For scorners delight in their scorning, And fools hate knowledge." Through my spiritual journey, I have become aware of the fact that all persons operating outside of the kingdom of God fall into this dysfunctional category. Our calling is different: "But God chose the foolish things of the world to shame the wise; God chose the weak things of the world to shame the strong" (1 Cor. 1:27, NIV).

It is very unfortunate that many of us only turn to God during adversity. During these periods we are looking for God to give us an instant fix. When we do not obtain an immediate response to our prayers, we become despondent, impatient, and ultimately create a wrong solution. Only with the truth of God do we align to His solutions and create kingdom outcomes.

In search of kingdom truth, I have learned many things. What stands out very clearly is that extraordinary achievements only come from God. Extraordinary achievement by the world's standard is temporal and at times meaningless. However, when we experience extraordinariness from God, it not only lasts through Earth's transient moment but extends into eternity.

What would you consider to be extraordinary in your life? *Dictionary. com* defines *extraordinary* as "exceptional in character, amount, extent, degree, etc.; noteworthy; remarkable."[1] I have had the word *extraordinary* in my thoughts and heart for as long as I am able to remember. However, only since I met our Creator did I truly know that I am able to accomplish extraordinary things in Him. Prior to my encounter with God, I believed that being extraordinary referred to worldly achievements such as education, wealth, career, position, and social status. I have since learned that these are only minor accomplishments in the grand scope of the kingdom of God. Extraordinariness only comes from one's awareness of the presence and power of the Spirit of God within us. Specifically, it refers to those who are wise enough to accept Jesus as Lord and Savior. Nothing on this earth and in this life—not wealth, education, status, or anything else—matters more than to have a personal, intimate relationship with our Creator. A daily dosage of God's Word provides wisdom, knowledge, increases faith and character, and is paramount to accomplish the extraordinary. How would you like to find the tool to conquer your perils? Become obsessed with God, and He will turn all your perils into opportunities that will change your life forever.

Take delight in the LORD, and He will give your heart's desires.
                                                            —PSALM 37:4

I have never met a Christian, or a non-believer for that matter, who enjoys the experience of adversity. Fortunately, as Christians, we have been given access to the tools and resources to conquer such challenges. The Word of God conquers all. However, I would venture to say that many believers would be unsuccessful with the tool, if called to use it. Many attend church; however, the extent of their biblical knowledge and study is linked merely to the sermon. In many instances, if asked about the biblical components of the sermon, they would not be able to share the content with others. This is where many of us need to change. In order to use God's tools to overcome our perils, we need to study to become knowledgeable about His Word.

In order to have true fellowship with God, we must walk in the light, as He is in the light. You might ask, What would that fellowship look like? It is an activity that requires participation from you and the Spirit within you. We must spend time in the Word to develop the relationship, and then the Spirit of God will commence the process of cleansing, followed by discernment. As we walk in love, faith, and obedience, God adds more knowledge and increases our blessings and usefulness for service. How? When we study and meditate on the Word, He turns on the light to revelation, which leads us to discernment of His will.

Unfortunately for the non-believers, they have forfeited the truth of the gospel of Jesus Christ and rebelled against God. They have chosen the world's ungodly ways. Hence, our heavenly Father respects the free will He has given and has allowed them to proceed independently.

God Uses People to Accomplish
His Will for Humanity

People of all levels are used by God to accomplish His will in the Earth's realm. The following individuals accomplished the extraordinary because the all listened to God and followed the promptings of His Spirit.

Four hundred years ago, William Tyndale embraced his heavenly assignment and translated considerable parts of the Bible into English for public lay readership.[2] Tyndale was the first to draw directly from Hebrew and Greek texts. He was also the first to take advantage of the new medium of print, which allowed for its wide distribution. Tyndale was accused of heresy, assassinated for obedience to his vision and defiance to the authority of the hierarchy of the Roman Catholic Church, and was unable to complete the assignment. However, like all else which comes from God, the baton was passed, and the original objective was accomplished. Obedience of this magnitude deserves far more attention than is given by the Christian community. Tyndale's commitment to this assignment is a clear indication that in translation of the Bible he provided a powerful resource to the Earth's population, one that the hierarchy of the Roman Catholic Church attempted to block to continue control over its flock. Fortunately for us, the church hierarchy was unsuccessful. The Bible is the only resource available in the Earth's realm to change lives. However, it will only work in the lives of those with the wisdom and courage to implement its content into their daily lives. Where would Christianity be today without access to the Word of God?

Martin Luther was the first leader to openly depart from the Roman Catholic Church. He did not intentionally set out to start his own church. Rather, he was committed to the call and sought discussion coupled with change. In his role as a German monk, he struggled to understand his relationship to God.[3] He eventually concluded that he was not worthy of approaching God. Therefore, he reasoned that salvation was neither deserved nor earned but was solely a gift of grace from God.

Luther discovered something that led him to make several critiques of the Roman Catholic Church. He discovered the selling of indulgences by the hierarchy of the Catholic Church, which he audaciously exposed. On October 31, 1517, Martin Luther tacked his Ninety-Five Theses to the church door at Wittenberg, in Saxony, Germany.

The following were some of the major points in the document:

Luther emphasized the doctrine of justification by grace through faith. The emphasis on faith alone was a significant shift in perspective. In particular, it undercut the selling of "indulgences," artifacts sold by the church as symbols of religious devotion. [The faithful were encouraged to purchase these indulgences from the church in exchange for prayers that their deceased loved ones would receive forgiveness of the sins they committed while alive.] By criticizing this practice Luther challenged an important source of revenue for the church.

Pushed by the church hierarchy and backed by some of the German nobility, Luther rejected the authority of the Pope. He suggested that the Bible alone should be the guide for Christian Life, and that German Christians did not need to listen (or pay taxes!) to the Pope in Italy.

Luther also disagreed with the idea that priest were needed to approach God on behalf of the people. Rather, he proposed a priesthood of all believers, saying that people could communicate with God directly.

Luther insisted that the church should use the common language of the people, and not Latin as was the practice in the Roman Catholic tradition. As a result, Luther led mass in German and even translated the entire Bible into this European language.[4]

God is looking for men and women who will read His Word and not be complacent regarding discovery, discernment, or revelation received. The will of God is to get gospel of truth into every remote corner of the Earth, free of deceit or gimmicks.

George Washington Carver was another example of a man with a hungry heart for God. Carver tapped into the Spirit of God within him from an early age. He learned to talk to God. The Bible was his source of direction and he gave God the glory for all his scientific successes. Henry Madison Morris writes, "Carver was also a sincere and humble Christian, never hesitating to confess his faith in the God of the Bible and attributing all his success and ability to God. In 1939 [Carver] was awarded the Roosevelt medal, with the following citation: 'To a scientist humbly seeking the guidance of God and a liberator to men of the white race as well as the black.'"[5] The following are excerpts from George Washington Carver's writings, in his own words and with the original spelling and grammar preserved:

My sister mother and myself were *ku klucked,* and sold in *Arkansaw* and there are now so many conflicting reports concerning them I dare not say if they are dead or alive. Mr. Carver the jentleman who owned my mother sent a man for us, but only I was brought back, nearly dead with whooping cough with the report that mother & sister was dead, although some sauy they saw them afterwards going north with the soldiers.

My home was near Neosho Newton Co Missouri where I remained until I was about 9 years old my body was very feble and it was a constant warfare between life and death to see who would gain the mastery...

I was just a mere boy when converted, hardly ten years old. There isn't much of a story to it. God just came into my heart one afternoon while I was alone in the "loft" of our big barn while I was shelling corn to carry to the mill to be ground into meal. A dear little white boy, one of our neighbors, about my age came by one Saturday morning, and in talking and playing he told me he was going to Sunday school tomorrow morning. I was eager to know what a Sunday school was. He said they sang hymns and prayed. I asked him what prayer was and what they said. I do not remember what he said; only remember that as soon as he left I climbed up into the "loft," knelt down by the barrel of corn and prayed as best I could. I do not remember what I said. I only recall that I felt so good that I prayed several times before I quit. My favorite song was "Must Jesus Bear the Cross Alone and all the world go free," etc.

At the age of 10 years, I left for Neosho, a little town just 8 miles from our farm, where I could go to school. Mr. and Mrs. Carver were perfectly willing for us to go where we could be educated the same as white children. I remained here about two years, got an opportunity to go to Fort Scott, Kansas with a family. Every year I went to school, supporting myself by cooking and doing all kinds of house work in private families.

After finishing my Bachelor's degree I was elected a member of the faculty, and given charge of the greenhouse, bacteriological laboratory, and the laboratory work in systematic botany. Mr. Washington said he needed a man of my training. I accepted and came to Tuskegee, and have been here ever since.

I am more and more convinced, as I search for truth that no ardent student of nature, can "Behold the lillies of the field"; or

"Look unto the hills", or study even the microscopic wonders of a stagnant pool of water, and honestly declare himself to be an Infidel. More and more as we come closer and closer in touch with nature and its teachings are we able to see the Divine and are therefore fitted to interpret correctly the various languages spoken by all forms of nature about us.

My life time study of nature in it's many phazes leads me to believe more strongly than ever in the Biblical account of man's creation as found in Gen. 1:27 "And God created man in his own image, in the image of God created He him; male and female created he them.' Of course sciences [sic] through all of the ages have been searching for the so-called "missing link" which enables us to interpert man from his very beginning, up to his present high state of civilization. I am fearful lest our finite researches will be wholly unable to grasp the infinite details of creation, and therefore we lose the great truth of the creation of man.[6]

It is very ironic that George Washington Carver was God's instrument for many scientific discoveries. However, sadly enough, so many of our educators deemed this unimportant. They failed to reveal to their students the true source of Carver's scientific discoveries and successes. Out of my own curiosity, I have interviewed a few dozen students regarding the topic. My question to them was, Were you ever taught about who or what was the source of George Washington Carver's discovery in school? There was not even one affirmative answer from these students. Why? Perhaps the laws have separated God from our education system and have prevented teaching of highly relevant and beneficial information. For this reason, it is ever more important that parents take on the role of teaching their children about God. Think for a moment. Without insight and teaching on this important topic, our children will always look to mere man for enlightenment. They will always look to mere man to emulate and use as role models. We are responsible for the education of our children. (Suggested reading for additional information regarding Carver's spirituality and Godly insight: Glenn Clark's *Man Who Talks With the Flowers*.)

William Tyndale, Martin Luther, and George Washington Carver were individuals who discovered their purpose. They were fortunate to have discovered their true Source in life. They elected to honor God and follow Spirit guidance to accommodate His will for humanity. We would never have obtained insight into the workings of the Spirit of God without account of significant contributors like these and others in the Bible. Are you willing to listen for the call from God and follow through with the promptings of the Spirit? Think of what this world would be like today if every household used the Bible as their guide, as was originally intended. Our world would be one without injustice, prejudice, or greed. The Holy Spirit would continuously convict us of wrongdoing toward others. We would operate from love, honor, and a reverence for God.

Jesus came into to the Earth's realm in the likeness of man. He humbled Himself and became obedient to the point of death. He was sent from heaven to Earth to fulfill a mission of utmost importance. We have been given the same authority Jesus had. Therefore, with faith and obedience we are able to accomplish the will of God for our lives. God has given every believer the power to bring the unseen into the realm of the seen. Our ultimate is to replicate what Jesus did in our own lives.

God said, "Let there be light" (Gen. 1:3)—and it was! Since we are made in His image, we were created with the same ability and power. We must take the time to educate ourselves on the rules of the kingdom of God's constitution, one that supersedes Earth's. Then we would operate from a superior law and, hence, develop higher standards. We were given the tool to accomplish God's will in our lives. What is holding you back from your part?

GOD'S WORD MAKES FAITH

The entire universe came into existence by faith at God's command.

> What is faith? It is the confident assurance that what we hope for is going to happen. It is the evidence of things we cannot yet see…It is impossible to please God without faith. Anyone who wants to come to Him must believe that there is a God and that he rewards those who sincerely seek him.
> —HEBREWS 11:1, 6

When we study the events in the Bible it helps us to understand how God operated in the past and what we can count on Him to do in our lives today. For example, consider one of the stories of Moses. The events that set Israel apart as a nation occurred because of Moses' obedience. God despises any form of injustice. Pharaoh, the king of Egypt, committed a great deal of atrocities against the Hebrew people, and as a result, God enlisted Moses with an assignment to free the people.

One day Moses was tending the flock of his father-in-law, Jethro, the priest of Midian, and he went deep into the wilderness near Sinai, the mountain of God. Suddenly, the angel of the LORD appeared to him as a blazing fire in a bush. Moses was amazed because the bush was engulfed in flames, but it didn't burn up. "Amazing!" Moses said to himself. "Why isn't that bush burning up? I must go over to see this." When the LORD saw that he had caught Moses' attention, God called to him from the bush, "Moses! Moses!" "Here I am!" Moses replied. "Do not come any closer," God told him. "Take off your sandals, for you are standing on holy ground." Then he said, "I am the God of your ancestors—the God of Abraham, the God of Isaac, and the God of Jacob." When Moses heard this, he hid his face in his hands because he was afraid to look at God. Then the LORD told him, "You can be sure I have seen the misery of my people in Egypt. I have heard their cries for deliverance from their harsh slave drivers. Yes, I am aware of their suffering. So I have come to rescue them from the Egyptians and lead them out of Egypt into their own good and spacious land. It is a land flowing with milk and honey—the land where the Canaanites, Hittites, Amorites, Perizzites, Hivites, and Jebusites live. The cries of the people of Israel have reached me, and I have seen how the Egyptians have oppressed them with heavy tasks. Now go, for I am sending you to Pharaoh. You will lead my people, the Israelites, out of Egypt."

—EXODUS 3:1–10

Initially, Moses protested. "Who am I to appear to before Pharaoh?...How can you expect me to lead the Israelites out of Egypt?" (Exod. 3:11). God's response was, "I will be with you" (v. 12). I believe that every believer who has ever been tapped for an assignment from God is able to relate to the feeling of not being qualified. Moses took the first step. He returned to Egypt to lead the Israelites to freedom from bondage. Pharaoh's organization was a new regime, which made it bit safer. Moses' response to God's assignment to lead the Israelites to freedom was a demonstration and later manifestation of how the Lord needs believers like us to accomplish His will on the Earth. The plagues placed upon Egypt because of Pharaoh's refusal to let the Hebrew people go were a demonstration of the perils created from disobedience to God. Moses' courage opened our eyes as to what can be accomplished in obedience. The Israelites walked across the Red Sea on dry ground to arrive at Mt. Sinai, where God gave the Ten Commandments.

God is the same yesterday, today, and will be tomorrow. What He did back then, He is able to do again today. Before any of these promises in the Bible can come to fruition, we need to open the Book, gain wisdom, and come into the light of God. Our treasures in God have been deposited in the Guidebook. Because many are not reading the Book, they are poverty-stricken in spite of all the money they profess to have. (In this case, poverty is not about lack of money.) We need to pray for discernment so that we might claim our treasure in God's Word.

We express love in our relationships with gifts and attention, and God expresses His with biblical promises in His Word. God is true to His promise, and believers are given full authority to claim all when the context of Scripture allows it. God requires that we believe in His promises when we are confronted with difficulties. God wants to give us good and much more. However, the kingdom promises are not automatic. They require adherence to the rules.

The more we read the Bible and understand God's ways and promises, the more prayer protection we are able to provide to our love ones when required. The more we know, the more confident we become. Faith and trust increases as we study God's Word. Here is what God said He would do for the children of those who honor Him.

> Happy are those who fear the LORD. Yes, happy are those who delight in doing what he commands. Their children will be successful everywhere; an entire generation of godly people will be blessed.
> —PSALM 112:1–2

Is it not worth it to protect your children? This is a promise that I have believed and claimed in my own life, and God honored it. Why would we not want to adhere to it and receive blessing from His covenant promises? It would be considered unwise for anyone not to get on board so that their loved ones will remain under God's protective shield.

GOD HONORS FAITH

We can only exercise faith when we know God's Word. If we do not know the Word, on what do we base our faith? Ordinarily, the world's darkness is the other alternative.

On June 4, 2004, my daughter was scheduled for a routine surgery at a hospital. It was a Friday morning, and I accompanied her to the hospital. She was supposed to return home later that day. However, her discharge was delayed because of surgical complications. During surgery, she developed an air embolism. This condition caused her to stop breathing on her own. She was placed on a respirator for approximately twenty-six hours. After twelve hours I was advised by the head of anesthesiology that I should call the chaplain, as they did not believe she would make it. The doctor stated that if she did come out of it, she would suffer brain damage. Had I not known the Word of God, I would have succumbed to the frailty of humans and not the supernatural power of the Creator of the universe.

Based on what I had learned from my study and meditation in the Bible, I knew that whatever words I uttered would determine the outcome of my daughter's situation. I turned to the head of anesthesiology and I said, "My daughter is fine. No need for a chaplain." And I proceeded to the Chapel to pray on my own. Here is what I said in prayer: "God, I surrender her to You. She is Your creation. I know You love her way more than I do. She was Yours first, and You gave her to me. You said in Your Word that '[Jesus] took our sicknesses and removed our diseases' (Matt. 8:17). 'You have seen well, for I am ready to perform My word' (Jer. 1:12, NKJV). 'Jesus looked at them and said, "With men it is impossible, but not with God; for with God all things are possible"' (Mark 10:27, NKJV)." I concluded by saying, "I receive that covenant promise by faith. I thank You for it, and I give You all the glory in Jesus' name. Amen." I spent the rest of the time in thanksgiving for the miracle I knew that God would perform. Mentally, I kept these promises in my heart as I meditated the entire time.

I went back to her room and remained there in faith that God would do what the Word said He would do. Later that day—I remember so clearly as if it were yesterday—I sat next to my daughter in the room and was holding her hand, and she opened her eyes. I thanked God as I knew all was well. The doctors were stunned. Because of their conclusion, they prepared for the necessary tests to ensure no brain damage, and there was none. Kimberly was released during the next couple of days and has never been back with any issue from that incident. Today she is healthy and back in her law practice. Had I not known the Word, I would have opened my mouth, said the wrong thing, and changed the entire outcome.

We must wake up to the laws given in the Guidebook. God is the power, not the doctors. They are only His instruments. Once we accept Jesus, He has given us authority to come to Him with our prayer of petition, but if you do not read the Bible you will not be able to discover and claim those promises—and God takes delight in blessing us.

In another incident in the summer of 2008, my daughter was returning home in her car from dinner with friends when she was hit from the rear. Her car spun around, and she was pushed into oncoming traffic. Just picture this scenario: driving a sports car with the top down, being thrust into oncoming traffic. Had there been any cars coming, she would likely have been ejected from the vehicle. Instead, there was no traffic in the normally busy intersection, and she was protected by an angel of the Lord. God's power works, and those who abide in His Word receive the benefit of His blessing from His promises. That night, five people were taken to the hospital with injuries. However, my daughter was unscathed. She was the only one who had not been hurt. Her car was totaled, but that was the extent of it.

On that particular Saturday, the Lord was dealing with me about prayer in the Spirit, and I spent many hours at it. In hindsight He was paving the way for what was coming later with discernment, meditation, and prayer. This incident was a supernatural manifestation of God's Word and power.

Many have opened themselves to the tricks of the devil because they have refused to make the Word of God the final authority in their lives. When trouble comes, the question is always why God allowed this or that to happen. He gave us the Guidebook; when we choose to ignore it, we remove His protective shield from the situation. He gave us the power, and by ignoring it we allow harm to come upon us, not Him. It is vital that those of us in the body of Christ become familiar with kingdom resources for protection. I am very fortunate that my daughter knew about the use of the Word of God as a resource of protection.

> Fight the good fight of faith for what we believe. Hold tightly to the eternal life that God has given you, which you have confessed so well before many witnesses.
>
> —1 Timothy 6:12

Align Behavior as You Learn

As I developed in understanding, I realized that most of the adversities I experienced were created from my thoughts, words, and/or deeds. When we know the content of the Bible we commence to guard our mouths, as every spoken word has the potential to create either a peril or a blessing. The Bible states that what goes in to a man's mouth does not make him unclean. It is what comes out of his mouth that damages him (Matt. 15:11). The things that go into the mouth go into the stomach and come out of the body, while those that come out of the mouth are released from the heart and defile a man. Out of the mouth comes evil, adultery, murder, sexual immorality, false testimony, greed, and slander. These are what make a man unclean. Pay attention to the words you speak.

As a part of the Body of Christ, I believe it is each of our responsibility to ensure effectiveness in all areas of God's mandate. It is our individual words and actions that lead His people to the kingdom, as our distinctive effort helps to accomplish the whole purpose of God. The Body of Christ should always be more advanced than the secular world in all areas. We are the leaders. Let us start to take our role seriously and refrain from acting as mere followers, lest we fall into the pit with everyone else.

Here is what God said regarding our spoken word: "Now tell them this: 'As surely as I live, I will do to you the very things I heard you say. I, the LORD, have spoken!'" (Num. 14:28). He had heard all that the Israelites had been saying. This also applies to us today. I sometimes cringe when I listen to the things that come from the mouths of Christians. Here are some examples of words that defeat people: "These shoes are killing me"; "My vision is getting bad"; "I am getting old and cannot remember"; "I am broke"; "I will probably get diabetes, high blood pressure, and cancer"; "It runs in my family"; "I might never get out of debt"; "I will never find a job"; "The economy is getting worse"; "I believe I am going to catch a cold". It is amazing how unaware most believers are. Like children we need to understand that when we speak truth our heavenly Father is able to manifest the Word.

> So also, the tongue is a small thing, but what enormous damage it can do. A tiny spark can set a great forest on fire. And the tongue is a flame of fire. It is full of wickedness that can ruin your whole life. It can turn the entire course of your life into a blazing flame of destruction, for it is set on fire by hell itself.
>
> —JAMES 3:5–6

The words we speak determine our destiny.

As I matured in character, I surrendered as clay in the hands of a master potter to my heavenly Father to allow Him to shape my steps into His will. My responsibility is to remain in surrender and allow Him to shape me into the image of His Son, something that can be used to accomplish His plan here on Earth. When we neglect reading the Bible, our spirit misses the nourishment required. The Spirit of God within suffers in the same manner that the body, the flesh, deteriorates without food to maintain health. When a person is born again from above, the Son of God is born within, and that life starves without the daily nourishment of the Word. I endeavor to surrender and be led by the Spirit of God within.

I am now in a place of catch-up, as I still intend to receive all that God planned for me before His creation. According to scripture, the Lord says, "I will give you back what you lost to the stripping locusts, the cutting locusts, the swarming locusts, and the hopping locusts. It was I who send this great destroying army against you" (Joel 2:25). I lost blessings because of ignorance to the Word of God.

I have done a great deal of study and have realized that believers do not explore the benefits given to us as the body of Christ. It is so much more than a weekly visit to a church, the building. I do not suggest that anyone discontinue that practice. However, we must couple the activity with study and meditation on the Word of God. To develop a relationship with God, we need to spend time communing with Him, and that is only done through the use of the Bible, our guide. Life is meant to be connected to God's force of power and authority, which is released when we speak His words.

This scripture completely resonates in my heart:

> "This is the new covenant I will make with my people on that day, says the Lord: I will put my laws in their hearts so they will understand them, and I will write them on their minds so they will obey them." Then he adds, "I will never again remember their sins and lawless deeds." Now when sins have been forgiven, there is no need to offer any more sacrifices.
> —Hebrews 10:16–18

What an awesome privilege to have complete and total access to the Creator of the universe deep within our inner being. Would you not agree that a commitment to this eternal covenant promise in the Bible is worth adhering to? The creative power that was born when God said, "Let there be light" (Gen. 1:3) was placed in the believer's heart at the moment Jesus was received as our Lord and Savior. That is a most spectacular revelation.

The Bible Offers Fail-proof Living

To desire to obey God, we need to know Him. Would you marry someone you did not know? Then how is it possible that most of us refuse to get to know our Creator intimately, when we were created to be in relationship with Him? The Lord is committed to transforming us. He has exclusive plans for us. However, He requires our cooperation. If we abide, I assure you that absolutely nothing will thwart the plan He predestined before the world began. His perfect will in our lives is to do His will. How? Read the Word and listen!

Many will not hear God when He gives them an assignment, because they have not met Him and are unfamiliar with the content of the Bible. Access is gained through spirit connection. How? Connection opens when the Father's Spirit intertwines with ours by way of the Word and provides us with discernment. The challenge for many of us is that we attempt to understand God through the world's broken system instead of the Word. Obedience to the Word of God gives birth to His blessing. Likewise, disobedience and ignorance hinders that blessing. The blessing is blocked because of sin (Gen. 3).

What kind of struggles have you been confronted with lately? The Bible is the resource that has been in existence for four hundred years, used not only to conquer the tricks and adversaries of the devil but for every adversity we will ever be confronted with. You might ask what devil you are referring to.

If you have no concept of an adversary in your life and in the earth's realm, then it might be difficult to derive benefit from this book. The adversary or the devil is that prompting within us that leads us to darkness and brings about evil.

Many people find Christians who do the Word of God a bit unrealistic or perhaps naive. But they are not naïve. They believe the Word and have seen God in action. Therefore, they are very confident in that revelation. It is very difficult for unbelievers to conceive that the Bible speaks truth. Scripture states, "I will destroy the wisdom of the wise; the intelligence of the intelligent I will frustrate" (1 Cor. 1:19, NIV). What they are not aware of is that God performs His Word with belief, faith, trust, and obedience. In the absence of those, skeptics will remain in darkness and be burdened by the tricks of the devil. When God's Word is the final authority in our lives, we are able to make an extraordinary impact for His kingdom. How so? We receive discernment and are able to respond to the call. We are all used as instruments to accommodate God's purposes. To receive discernment from the kingdom, God requires total commitment to the mandates in the Bible.

When we spend enough time in God's Word, He gives us revelation. The first thing we should do when we are confronted with a problem, instead of seeking the advice of friends, is to turn to God's Word. Open the Bible and search for scriptures concerning the issue at hand. Once you locate scriptures pertaining to that issue, study and meditate on them.

If you have a financial issue, here is a declaration based on Scripture that you might want to consider: "I believe God shall supply all my needs according to his riches and glory in Christ Jesus." (See Philippians 4:19.)

If you want to know why you were saved:

> He saved us, not because of the good things we did, but because of his mercy. He washed away our sins and gave us a new life through the Holy Spirit.
>
> —TITUS 3:5–6

If you want to know about love:

> For God so loved the world that he gave his only Son, so that everyone who believes in him will not perish but have eternal life.
>
> —JOHN 3:16

Want to know about our responsibility:

> Teach your children to choose the right path, and when they are older, they will remain upon it.
>
> —PROVERBS 22:6

If you want to know how you must live:

> And you must commit yourselves wholeheartedly to these commands I am giving you today. Repeat them again and again to your children. Talk about them when you are at home and when you are away on a journey, when you are lying down and when you are getting up again. Tie them to your hands as a reminder, and wear them on your forehead. Write them on the doorposts of your house and on your gates.
>
> —DEUTERONOMY 6:6–9

If you want to know about obedience:

> Today I am giving you a choice between a blessing and a curse! You will be blessed if you obey the commands of the LORD your God that I am giving you today. You will receive a curse if you reject the commands of the LORD your God and turn from his way by worshiping foreign gods.
>
> —DEUTERONOMY 11:26–28

If you want to know about spiritual warfare:

> Be strong with the Lord's mighty power. Put on all of God's armor so that you will be able to stand firm against all strategies and tricks of the Devil. For we are not fighting against people made of flesh and blood, but against the evil rulers and authorities of the unseen world…against wicked spirits in the heavenly realms.
>
> —EPHESIANS 6:10–12

If you want to know about discipleship:

> Jesus came and told his disciples, "I have been given complete authority in heaven and on earth. Therefore, go and make disciples of all the nations, baptizing them in the name of the Father and the Son and the Holy Spirit. Teach these new disciples to obey the commands I have given you. And be sure of this: I am with you always, even to the end of the age.
>
> —MATTHEW 28:18–20

If you want to know about rebellion to God:

> But God shows his anger from heaven against all sinful, wicked people who push the truth away from themselves. For the truth about God is known to them instinctively. God has put this knowledge in their hearts. From the time the world was created, people have seen the earth and sky and all that God made. The can clearly see his invisible qualities—his eternal power and divine nature. So they have no excuse whatsoever for not knowing God.
>
> —ROMANS 1:18–20

If you want to know God's will for your life:

> When the Spirit of truth comes, he will guide you into all truth. He will not be presenting his own ideas; he will be telling you what he has heard. He will tell you about the future. He will bring me glory by revealing to you whatever he receives from me.
>
> —JOHN 16:13–14

NOURISH YOUR SPIRIT WITH THE WORD OF GOD

God needs to get our thinking in line with His Word so that we might be useful for the kingdom. How so? Without an adherence and attention to a call, God does not get His will done in the earthly realm. We are the hands of God on Earth. It is important for us to yield and not object to the fingers He uses to shape our character. His purpose is to rid us from our carnal ways so that we might experience fullness of life in Jesus Christ.

When all else fails, the Word of God is eternal, and it will always remain. God is Spirit, and He is able to come into our heart and guide us through every difficult situation we experience. We are unable to conquer addictive behavior, such as alcohol abuse, drugs, smoking, sex, and so forth in our own strength. However, with the Spirit of God within, all is conquerable.

If God is not in our lives, we are not living; we merely exist. Wholeness and peace come from Him. No one is able to discern this from someone else. It is only revealed through salvation, the desires of the heart, and belief in the Word of God. For a follower of Jesus, death is nothing more than a transition from Earth's temporal realm to God's eternal kingdom. As for me, my commitment is unshakable, and I will share this message with anyone who is wise enough to receive it.

> For the word of God is full of living power. It is sharper than the sharpest knife, cutting deep into our innermost thoughts and desires. It exposes us for what we really are.
> —Hebrews 4:12

> From eternity to eternity I am God. No one can oppose what I do. No one can reverse my actions.
> —Isaiah 43:13

Think for a moment. Look at the state of the world we live in, the things that are happening all around us. War, famine, earthquakes, genocide, and tsunamis are taking place on a daily basis. Is it not worth it to make an effort to give the Bible an opportunity to change your life? Try it; I assure you a change in your thinking will be evident after thirty days of reading. If this does not happen, all you have lost is thirty days of reading God's Word. However, it might just change your life from a world of darkness into an eternal life of light, love, and peace.

Here is an action that you might consider that worked for me: the Book of Proverbs has thirty-one days. Start with reading one a day, and it will provide you with practical instruction for successful wisdom living in the kingdom of God. Proverbs teaches special wisdom revealed by God, as well as common sense, both of which must play a role in our lives in order to be successful. Once I did this for a month, I noticed that I started to align my mind to the Word. It is our mind that affects the world outside of us. Repetition of the Scriptures for six months changed my thought pattern completely and brought it into alignment with the Word. This happened exactly as God said it would. Supernaturally, the Spirit worked and renewed my mind: "Instead, there must be a spiritual renewal of your thoughts and attitudes. You must display a new nature because you are a new person, created in God's likeness—righteous, holy, and true" (Eph. 4:23–24).

In the same manner in which we provide our bodies with daily sustenance, we need to provide our spirit with God's Word. Spirit food is the Word of God. The unbeliever is unable to get a glimpse of the power of our Creator unless there is a repentant heart and complete acceptance of Jesus as Lord. They will never experience total light, but instead they will live in a state of perpetual darkness. God is no respecter of persons. What He does for one He will do for all. However, we must be in compliance with the laws established in the Bible. God loves all of humanity. However, He will only reveal Himself to those who love Him and obey His teachings. Individuals who receive Jesus welcome the One who sent Him into the world. It is love that releases power. Without it, we are spiritually dead, separated from God and His provisions. We are all walking around with authority in the power of the almighty God inside of us. However, we will not get a taste of it unless we walk with Him.

The plans created by man will never measure up to the ones prepared and preordained by our heavenly Father. He arranged these plans for us before the beginning of the world. Submit, trust, have faith, and be open to receive what is a part of your kingdom, eternal inheritance. Earthly legacies of wealth are all temporal and do not receive credits in the kingdom. A newborn child raised on the biblical principles of the Word of God will by far supersede the actions, values, and character of a new child born into wealth and trained under man's earthly, ungodly way of doing things. Under the guidance of biblical upbringing, the fruit of the Holy Spirit is the controlling force.

> But when the Holy Spirit controls our lives, he will produce this kind of fruit in us: love, joy, peace, patience, kindness, goodness, faithfulness, gentleness, and self-control. Here there is no conflict with the law.
>   —GALATIANS 5:22–23

On the contrary, under the guidance of the world's upbringing, the devil controls the outcome.

Don't be misled. Remember that you can't ignore God and get away with it. You will always reap what you sow! Those who live only to satisfy their own sinful nature will harvest the consequences of decay and death. But those who live to please the Spirit will harvest everlasting life from the Spirit.

—Galatians 6:7–8

World Creation

There is nothing created in this world that did not come from God. In the beginning the Word already existed; it was with God and was Him. Not one thing in all creation was finished without Him. The Word is the source of life to all people. Light shined in obscurity, and the darkness has never put it out. Those who believed in the light were given the right to become God's children.

Sin creates darkness and brings about evil. Read the account of Lucifer's fall. The first sin ever committed was pride, the desire to acquire wisdom independent from God (Isa. 14:12–15). The sin of pride that led to Satan's demise had now tainted the hearts and minds of Adam and Eve in the Earth's realm. God's command in the Garden of Eden was to not eat from the tree of good and evil.

It's only the fruit from the tree at the center of the garden that we are not allowed to eat. God says we must not eat it or even touch it, or we will die.

—Genesis 3:3

Satan deceived Eve to think that she could be like God if she ate from the tree of good and evil. Adam followed, and human sin entered the world (Gen. 3:1–6).

Satan's plot to deceive Eve was the most significant event of all time. Because of the success of Satan's plot, we all came into the world with a sinful nature, and God was forced to institute a new plan for humanity's redemption, the crucifixion of Jesus Christ. Jesus came and took upon Himself the sin of the entire human race and reestablished our redemption. Only when we accept Him as Savior can we receive salvation. If there were no power in God's Word we could not be born again. Salvation is a free gift, and there is nothing we need to do to earn it. In God's love and grace we are all entitled to it. All we need to do is receive it.

Not knowing why we were created perpetuates our state of oppression from freedom and incompletion. No one is able to make another complete but the Spirit of God within. We get in trouble when we believe that others are able to make us whole. Parents, spouses, children, or any other significant persons cannot accomplish completeness in our life. One of the ways we can manage the difficulties in our life is to embrace and claim God's Word in the Bible. God always keeps His promises. Having this revelation makes it easier to trust that He will do what He says. We have been given free will to choose light or darkness.

> Today I have given you the choice between life and death, between blessings and curses. I call on heaven and earth to witness the choice you make. Oh, that you would choose life, that you and your descendants might live! Choose to love the LORD your God and to obey him and commit yourself to him, for he is your life. Then you will live long in the land the LORD swore to give your ancestors Abraham, Isaac, and Jacob.
>
> —DEUTERONOMY 30:19–20

WE ARE ALL CHOSEN

God does not have favorites.

> For God does not show favoritism.
>
> —ROMANS 2:11

> I see very clearly that God doesn't show partiality.
>
> —ACTS 10:34

It is extremely important that this is clear in our mind and heart. Although salvation came through the Jews, many of them continue to be without their Messiah, blinded from truth and in unbelief. They neither understood nor recognized their Messiah. God chose Israel for a divine purpose. The Jewish population of believers were chosen and entrusted to take God's Word throughout the nations. However, many have been stuck in time with the Law of Moses, in defiance to God's assignment. Hence they were scattered throughout the Earth (Deut. 30:1–9).

> For the law was given through Moses; God's unfailing love and faithfulness came through Jesus Christ.
>
> —JOHN 1:17

Their unbelief sprouted from a story concocted by the Jewish religious leaders. This fabrication wreaked much havoc within a population of believers and has continued to this day. The Bible tells us:

> As the women were on their way into the city, some of the men who had been guarding the tomb went to the leading priests and told them what had happened. A meeting of all the religious leaders was called, and they decided to bribe the soldiers. They told the soldiers, "You must say, 'Jesus' disciples came during the night while we were sleeping, and they stole his body.' If the governor hears about it, we'll stand up for you and everything will be all right." So the guards accepted the bribe and said what they were told to say. Their story spread widely among the Jews, and they still tell it today. Then the eleven disciples left for Galilee, going to the mountain where Jesus had told them to go.
> —MATTHEW 28:11–16

Jewish people say, "We are Abraham's descendants." Indeed they are! However, many remain in unbelief and in slavery to sin just like all others who are in denial of Jesus, *Yeshua*, the Messiah, Son of the living God. They have a zeal for God, but it is a misdirected one. In ignorance to God's righteousness they seek to establish their own.

> For Christ has accomplished the whole purpose of the law. All who believe in him are made right with God.
> —ROMANS 10:4

Divine authority supersedes all religious traditions (Matt. 23:13). Scripture tells us no one can see the kingdom of God without being born again. You might wonder, How is someone born again? Jesus said:

> A person is born physically of human parents but is born spiritually of the Spirit. Do not be surprised...The wind blows wherever it wishes; you hear the sound it makes, nonetheless, you do not know where it comes from or where it is going. It is like that with everyone who is born of the Spirit.
> —JOHN 3:6–8

Without a true understanding of this, it becomes difficult to recognize our newness in Christ and activate our helper the Holy Spirit. Jesus said. "I am the resurrection and the life. Those who believe in me, even though they die like everyone else, will live" (John 11:25). The Father said, "And all who believe in God's Son have eternal life. Those who don't obey the Son will never experience eternal life, but the wrath of God remains upon them" (John 3:36).

There is a word of wisdom from Scripture for all those self-appointed Jewish religious leaders. The Law of Moses was a shadow of the things to come. Jesus came to do the will of God. The first covenant was not perfect and had to be changed with the new one, Jesus (Heb. 10:9). God has given us free will to accept or reject Him (Gal. 2:21).

> And now, look, your house is left to you empty. And you will never see me again until you say, "Bless the one who comes in the name of the Lord.
>
> —LUKE 13:35

> How terrible it will be for you experts in religious law! For you hide the key to knowledge from the people. You don't enter the Kingdom yourselves, and you prevent others from entering.
>
> —LUKE 11:52

THE CONSEQUENCE OF UNBELIEF

There will be judgment for unbelief. Those who do not believe have already been judged in that they are denied salvation until they confess their acceptance of Jesus Christ. Light has come into the world, but people continue to embrace darkness because their deeds are sinful and they do not wish to be exposed. No one can have anything unless God gives it. He who comes from above is greater than all who come from the world; they who are from the world can only speak of earthly matters. The one who God sent speaks truth, as God has given His Spirit. Whoever does not believe in the Son will not have eternal life. Many of us spend our earthly life working to buy things such as clothing, electronics, fine dining, furniture, equipment, and other personal belongings that become useless over time. Would it not serve us more to spend some time on things that are of eternal life, like God's Word?

> I assure you, those who listen to my message and believe in God who sent me have eternal life. They will never be condemned for their sins, but they have already passed from death into life.
>
> —JOHN 5:24

CREATURES OF HABIT

Many of us are creatures of habit. Because we like things that are familiar and find comfort and security in them, we remain as we are rather than make the changes necessary to improve ourselves.

Not to receive salvation, nor to have the ability to make withdrawals from our heavenly bank account, is quite a tragedy. Have you ever wondered what happens after you accept Jesus Christ as your Savior? Or, do you ever wonder what should happen to a person once they are saved? Many people become saved; however, once they are saved, they receive no explanation of the next steps to follow towards a relationship with God. Therefore they continue to live the same sinful life and there is very little or no display of the newness received in Christ. This makes it very difficult for others to become interested in joining the Body of Christ. Why? Onlookers do not see any newness in behavior that is different from the rest of the world. Salvation without renewed minds has no impact for the kingdom of God, because access to the promise is hindered. When we are saved, our lives need to emulate the new Spirit of Jesus now within us.

The Bible says.

> Once you were dead, doomed forever because of your many sins. You used to live just like the rest of the world, full of sin, obeying Satan, the mighty prince of the power of the air. He is the spirit at work in the hearts of those who refuse to obey God. All of us used to live that way, following the passions and desires of our evil nature. We were born with an evil nature, and we are under God's anger just like everyone else. But God is so rich in mercy, and he loved us so very much, that even when we were dead because of our sins, he gave us life when he raised Christ from the dead. (It is only by God's special favor that you have been saved!)
> —EPHESIANS 2:1–5

Christians very rarely receive the discipleship training required to live as children of God. After salvation, we become citizens of the kingdom of God, and we have access to the treasury that grace provides. But, without renewal of the mind, a Christian could receive salvation seven times over and never gain access to the promises that the grace of God provides. When we renew our mind with the Bible, we align our thoughts and words with that of our Creator. We say what He says about us. We develop knowledge of what the Word says until we receive it in our spirit and it manifests in our lives. In essence, what we are to do is imitate God.

If we receive salvation but never read the Bible, our focus remains on the ungodly things of the world we live in. We continue to have desires of the flesh, those instant gratifiers which are very short lived and could result in major irreversible consequences. Renewal of the mind to align with the Word creates the newness that is expected from salvation. God will continue to bless those who are called to His purpose.

> And we know that God causes everything to work for the good of those who love God and are called according to his purpose for them.
>
> —ROMANS 8:28

NEWNESS IN CHRIST

I never envisioned myself with the kind of passion for the Word of God that I have today. I guess I took God for granted for most of my life. Although I had experienced many adversities throughout the course my life it was not until I was faced with a situation where my livelihood disappeared that I turned to God in every way. I gave up trying to control and fix the problems in my life and passed the torch to God completely. In retrospect, I am glad for the discipline, coupled with understanding, because the Father now has my undivided attention. I see so many people facing some of the same difficulties in life that I have endured. However, so many are looking to the wrong source to resolve their issues. Humanity continually turns to mere man to satisfy needs that only our Creator is equipped to resolve. I wish I could show everyone, but only God has the power to do that. All I can say is, if you want to know God more intimately, commit spending time praying and reading His Word.

If I were told prior to ten years ago that I would write a book on this topic from the Word of God's perspective, I would have said, "Absolutely not." My main reason for this emphatic denial is that before I experienced numerous perils I was one of those who attended church once a week, and that was the extent of my commitment. I never desired additional development. Why? I never saw that Christianity had any special benefits until I got into the Word of God. I had a life-altering experience and chose God for solutions as my alternative to mere men. My time spent with God changed my life. Study, meditation, faith, and obedience to God catapulted my journey from religious activities into an intimate, personal relationship with Jesus Christ. When I started my quest to know God and revelation came forth, my passion, coupled with the need to know more, increased.

Before, the only scripture I read in the Bible was Psalm 23, which was the one I saw my Mom pray. When we do not read the Bible, we do not set the example for our offspring to read it, let alone make it final authority in their lives. Without the Word of God, we rob our children of kingdom wisdom, knowledge, and inheritance. If we miss this as parents, we have failed in our responsibility. No gift or financial inheritance would ever be a replacement to the Word of God in the lives of our children. We owe it to our children to send them into the world prepared with a fail proof resource that can assist them with dealing with the difficulties that they undoubtedly will face in life. The Word of God is the tool for success in life!

Environment Creates Outcomes

Are you in an environment conducive to your development? When we are unfamiliar with the content of the Bible it is impossible to measure development. Therefore, study God's Word to ensure that your teaching is conducive to development. We cannot develop spiritually without planting Word of God seeds in our heart. It is the only way.

> Beware of false prophets who come disguised as harmless sheep, but are really wolves that will tear you apart. You can detect them by the way they act, just as you can identify a tree by its fruit. You don't pick grapes from thornbushes, or figs from thistles. A healthy tree produces good fruit, and an unhealthy tree produces bad fruit. A good tree can't produce bad fruit, and a bad tree can't produce good fruit. So every tree that does not produce good fruit is chopped down and thrown into the fire. Yes, the way to identify a tree or a person is by the kind of fruit that is produced. Not all people who sound religious are really godly. They may refer to me as "Lord," but they still won't enter the Kingdom of Heaven. The decisive issue is whether they obey my Father in heaven. On judgment day many will tell me, "Lord, Lord, we prophesied in your name and cast out demons in your name and performed many miracles in your name." But I will reply, "I never knew you. Go away; the things you did were unauthorized."
>
> —Matthew 7:15–23

God is not interested is us making converts out of people. He is the only one with the power to convert people. God wants believers to share the gospel. The most logical place to produce a harvest would be to be in an environment where we are thought to align God's Word with our daily activity.

Years back, I found myself in a church where I received no spiritual growth. However, I was much too ignorant in the things of God to know the difference. The really scary side to this picture is that many of us have given the responsibility of our Christian education to pastors and teachers. The only way to be biblically enlightened is to get into the Bible ourselves. Enlightenment from the Holy Spirit is the most assured way to develop in God.

As parents we need to be more attentive to the spiritual development of our children. World leaders have decided that they are more qualified than God to educate them. Hence, they have banned any and all things pertaining to God from our educational system. It is imperative that those of us that make up the body of Christ take the leading role to ensure that truth is taught in our communities. When Christians are asked, Do you believe that the Bible is the infallible Word of God? the response is usually yes. However, they are not able to tell you why. The biggest danger to our children is that we send them to college or into the world with no biblical sustenance or ability to defend their faith.

I believe the major reason why many of our children go into the world unprepared to defend their faith is that they are taught religion instead of relationship. I grew up in the Roman Catholic Church. However, I spent a lot of years in ignorance because of doctrine. I attended weekly mass, as well as confession. I made first communion, confirmation, and practiced all the religious rituals, rosary prayers, and all else that Catholics prac-tice. However, I never received any real, substantive teaching. Salvation was never explained to me, and I had not received a Spirit birth; hence, I was never saved. Once I started my study with the help of the Holy Spirit, I was forced to not only leave but run from the Roman Catholic Church. There is so much fallacy being taught.

As an example, Why should any believer confess to a priest? Were we not given the authority to go directly to the Father in the name of Jesus? Priests have no more power or authority than a believer.

> I tell you the truth, anyone who has faith in me will do what I have
> been doing. He will do even greater things than these, because
> I am going to the Father. And I will do whatever you ask in my

name, so that the Son may bring glory to the Father. You may ask
me for anything in my name, and I will do it.

—John 14:12–14, niv

In my Catholic upbringing, there was a great deal of idol worship. For
example, we were taught to make a prayer of petition to the Virgin Mary
and other saints. I have since learned those types of prayers are a form of
idol worship. Prayers of petition to anyone other than God in the name of
Jesus constitute idol worship.

As parents, if we have not led our children to solid biblical teaching and
have not taught them the steps to develop a personal, intimate relationship with our Creator we have done them a great injustice. If the only thing
we do right for our children is to give them a solid Word of God education, then we have transported them into extraordinary, wisdom-based
living. If this job is done poorly, generations down the line will be impacted
negatively.

The kingdom of God was never taught in the church where I grew up,
but God has now given me the opportunity to make a difference in lives of
others. God has placed in our reach a priceless treasure. It is unfortunate
that many will miss it because of unbelief or being planted in the wrong
environment. Rebellion and a lack of personal accountability for our spiritual development has led us to become a society of followers in ignorance
to our real purpose on Earth. Christians are to be the salt of the Earth.
However, we have been in a state of complacency. We have diverted from
God's positioning system and succumbed to the world's wicked ways.

Thanks to an awakening from perils I am no longer in a state of ignorance or complacency to the Word of God. Many use the term *Christian*
loosely without a true understanding of the call. God's command to us concerning the Book and guide for life is this:

Study this Book of the Law continually. Meditate on it day and
night so you may be sure to obey all that is written in it. Only then
will you succeed. I command you—be strong and courageous! Do
not be afraid or discouraged. For the Lord your God is with you
wherever you go.

—Joshua 1:8–9

GOD'S WORD, THE NUMBER ONE
RESOURCE TO MANAGE PERILS

When confronted with difficulties we must look to the Source, the Creator of the universe. I have now shifted from the world system and have aligned with the kingdom of God's constitution. This means I am in the world but not of it. I do not allow the dictates of this system to determine how I live my life.

You might ask, How might we move to this system? Commit to seek all direction from the outlined Guidebook we received from our Creator. To get started, pretend that you have just accepted Jesus as your Savior. Start to act the way children do with their parents and lean on the Holy Spirit within to make your decisions, regardless of how unimportant you deem the choice to be. It requires you to be simple minded (e.g., ask for guidance in the selection of clothing for work, school, or all else). This helps to develop the childlike behavior that God wants from His children. Do not be afraid. You might feel silly initially. However, once you get into it, you will start to notice that He will drop the choice in your spirit (the heart), and you will know exactly what He wants you to do. You will start to learn and detect His inner voice.

> And so, my children, listen to me, for happy are all who follow my ways. Listen to my counsel and be wise. Don't ignore it. Happy are those who listen to me, watching for me daily at my gates, waiting for me outside my home! For whoever finds me finds life and wins approval from the LORD. But those who miss me have injured themselves. All who hate me love death.
> —PROVERBS 8:32–36

God's aim is to satisfy all needs including the ones that we consider trivial to take to Him. In prayer or otherwise, everything that affects us is important to God. You undoubtedly consider the needs and wants of your children important. The same applies to our heavenly Father. Here is the assurance He gave us:

> And this same God who takes care of me will supply all your needs from his glorious riches, which have been given to us in Christ Jesus.
> —PHILIPPIANS 4:19

Think of how children depend on their parents for all things one hundred percent of the time. In this same manner, our heavenly Father created us to be dependent on Him. He wants the responsibility for supplying of all our needs. Why would anyone deprive him of that? Commence to read the Guidebook for direction daily, not just when trouble comes. Treat God's Word the same way you treat eating to nourish your body. Develop a passion for things that are eternal, change your thought pattern, and turn your back on temporal pursuits and instant gratification. For those in church and not seeing results, step up your study of the Word. Church attendance does not equate to either Word of God knowledge or biblical development. Once one becomes enlightened about the truth, light, and the Spirit of God within, it becomes utterly impossible to remain the same.

Many of the adversities in our lives we create ourselves, and in the majority of cases they produce major heartbreaks, setbacks, and at times destruction to entire families. When we have negative thoughts or speak negative words, we open the door for those things to manifest in our lives. Think a bit about some of your difficulties in your life. I believe you will be able to trace them back to a thought, a conversation, and/or perhaps a spoken word.

> Those who love to talk will experience the consequences, for the tongue can kill or nourish life.
> —Proverbs 18:21

Our Creator, God almighty, has left us with a sixty-six book love letter for living wisely, the Bible. We have foolishly ignored its content, and instead we spend a great deal of our time in search of the advice of ungodly men and women, so-called experts in their respective fields, to make life decisions that only the Holy Spirit within is equipped to make. It is mind-boggling how we have so little regard for our heavenly Father's message but we so freely commit to abiding to directions authored by humanity—and we swear by the results. Our world population is also so caught up in religious activities and ignores the notion that the journey is intended to be one of an intimate, personal relationship with Jesus.

> This is what the Lord says: "Cursed are those who put their trust in mere humans and turn their hearts away from the Lord. They are like stunted shrubs in the desert, with no hope for the future. They will live in the barren wilderness, on the salty flats where no one lives. But blessed are those who trust in the Lord and have made the Lord

their hope and confidence. They are like trees planted along a river-bank, with roots that reach deep into the water. Such trees are not bothered by the heat or worried by long months of drought. Their leaves stay green, and they go right on producing delicious fruit. The human heart is most deceitful and desperately wicked. Who really knows how bad it is? But I know! I, the Lord, search all hearts and examine secret motives. I give all people their due rewards, according to what their actions deserve."

—Jeremiah 17:5–10

Discover True Wisdom

Humanity will never discover true wisdom without God. God may have to use a storm to get some of us from the harbor and on board the ship. Earthly education is necessary and required; however, we deceive ourselves when we believe that it is the only requirement for wisdom. It is the require-ment for knowledge to function within the Earth's realm, but it will not suffice beyond that. True wisdom only comes from God.

> For the wisdom of this world is foolishness in God's sight. As it is written: "He catches the wise in their craftiness"; and again, "The Lord knows that the thoughts of the wise are futile." So then, no more boasting about men! All things are yours, whether Paul or Apollos or Cephas or the world or life or death or the present or the future—all are yours, and you are of Christ, and Christ is of God.
>
> —1 Corinthians 3:19–23, niv

Believers belong to Christ, and Christ belongs to God. For that reason we all belong to God. Who do you belong to? Are you living according to God's wisdom or that of men?

When we seek the wisdom of God, the Word is the tool to provide understanding. When we get to know God, He reveals to us the purpose for our existence. One of the greatest blessings we should all seek is the wisdom of God.

This wisdom opens the door to three things:

+ Discernment: The Spirit within allows us to discern good from evil.

+ Favor: He allows blessing to come upon us. The favor is not earned; it is unmerited favor by grace.

✦ Anointing: Is the enablement of the Holy Spirit to perform our assignment. The fullness of God comes in the form of the anointing.

Wisdom is calling you now. Will you respond to the call?

Listen as wisdom calls out! Hear as understanding raises her voice! She stands on the hilltop and at the crossroads. At the entrance to the city, at the city gates, she cries aloud, "I call to you, to all of you! I am raising my voice to all people. How naive you are! Let me give you common sense. O foolish ones, let me give you understanding. Listen to me! For I have excellent things to tell you. Everything I say is right, for I speak the truth and hate every kind of deception. My advice is wholesome and good. There is nothing crooked or twisted in it. My words are plain to anyone with understanding, clear to those who want to learn. Choose my instruction rather than silver, and knowledge over pure gold. For wisdom is far more valuable than rubies. Nothing you desire can be compared with it. I, Wisdom, live together with good judgment. I know where to discover knowledge and discernment. All who fear the LORD will hate evil. That is why I hate pride, arrogance, corruption, and perverted speech. Good advice and success belong to me. Insight and strength are mine. Because of me, kings reign, and rulers make just laws. Rulers lead with my help, and nobles make righteous judgments. I love all who love me. Those who search for me will surely find me. Unending riches, honor, wealth, and justice are mine to distribute. My gifts are better than the purest gold, my wages better than sterling silver! I walk in righteousness, in paths of justice. Those who love me inherit wealth, for I fill their treasuries. The LORD formed me from the beginning, before he created anything else. I was appointed in ages past, at the very first, before the earth began. I was born before the oceans were created, before the springs bubbled forth their waters. Before the mountains and the hills were formed, I was born—before he had made the earth and fields and the first handfuls of soil. I was there when he established the heavens, when he drew the horizon on the oceans. I was there when he set the clouds above, when he established the deep fountains of the earth. I was there when he set the limits of the seas, so they would not spread beyond their boundaries. And when he marked off the earth's foundations, I was the architect at his side. I was his constant delight, rejoicing always in his presence.

And how happy I was with what he created—his wide world and all the human family! And so, my children, listen to me, for happy are all who follow my ways. Listen to my counsel and be wise. Don't ignore it. Happy are those who listen to me, watching for me daily at my gates, waiting for me outside my home! For whoever finds me finds life and wins approval from the LORD. But those who miss me have injured themselves. All who hate me love death."

—PROVERBS 8

SHARE THE MESSAGE

It is selfish for a believer to receive salvation and keep it a secret. We must share the message through discipleship. What is true discipleship? Discipleship is based on a total commitment to Jesus Christ. It is not following after a particular doctrine. Rather, it entails giving up our right to ourselves to God. This is voluntary assignment, which should only be done willingly. God has given us free will and never forces anyone to do anything. Our Creator is looking for doers of the Word, those who read the Word and implement it in their lives.

If anyone desires to come after Me, let him deny himself.

—LUKE 9:23, NKJV

Are you growing in your faith? Is your trust in God rising? Do you believe that God is answering your petitions? If yes, then it is your duty to share. Once we become enlightened about truth, then we have a responsibility to share the good news. For me, it was only when I studied and gained knowledge that I became confident with sharing His message. What message do we share? Truth is the gospel of Jesus Christ. It is the good news of Jesus and His offer of salvation through His death, burial, and resurrection given by grace to be received in faith (1 Cor. 15:1–4).

Before we are able to get to the point of discipleship and sharing, we have to experience the cost. A large crowd was following Jesus. He turned and said to them:

If you want to be my follower you must love me more than your own father and mother, wife and children, brothers and sisters—yes, more than your own life. Otherwise, you cannot be my disciple. And you cannot be my disciple if you do not carry your own cross and follow me. But don't begin until you count the cost. For who would begin construction of a building without first getting estimates and then checking to see if there is enough money to pay the bills? Otherwise, you might complete only the foundation before running out of funds. And then how everyone would laugh at you! They would say, "There's the person who started that building and ran out of money before it was finished!"

—Luke 14:26–30

When I started on this journey, I was extremely fortunate that one of my first in-depth studies was on the topic of considering the cost of discipleship. I attended a week-long study, and a member of our study shared his own personal experience and difficulties in surrendering his son to God's care. He said he had recently started growing in faith and had difficulties with the concept of complete submission to God. One day he was praying and the Spirit of God said to him, "You must release your son to me." God further stated to him, "You are obsessed with him. You need to trust Me. He belonged to Me first, and I gave him to you. Now release him back to Me." He shared that after that experience the grace of God took him to a level of faith and complete trust. He surrendered his son after that experience and had complete faith that God would take care of him. I also managed to successfully surrender the care of my daughter to God. This became doable for me because of that original and continued study, coupled with developing trust in God.

Awareness of biblical figures helps us to understand and grow faith in this area. God said to Abraham, "Take your son, your only son—yes, Isaac, whom you love so much—and go to the land of Moriah. Go and sacrifice him as a burnt offering on one of the mountains, which I will point out to you" (Gen. 22:2). Abraham trusted God, and he knew that if Isaac was killed God would be able to bring him back to life. Would you adhere to God's request and trust your loved ones to God?

God wants our complete trust in every area. Once we learn this, it becomes easier to release our loved ones to Him. After years of study, I am now at a point where I will do whatever is revealed to me. In 2008 I was about to get married. I had been divorced for thirty years, and God said, "No, not yet." Although, this was very difficult, it never crossed my mind to disobey. I knew if God said no it was because He has something magnificent in store for me. I discovered truth and was not about to give it up for any reason. Moreover, based on what I know, the only marriage worth having is a godly one, one in which God is priority for both parties in the marriage. If God is at the helm of any marriage, then love reigns, and the experience is bound to be heaven on Earth. Marriages should be made up of equally yoked individuals.

We are all accountable to God in every area of our lives, and most importantly we are to share the truth that has been given to us.

> Not all people who sound religious are really godly. They may refer to me as "Lord," but they still won't enter the Kingdom of Heaven. The decisive issue is whether they obey my Father in heaven. On judgment day many will tell me, "Lord, Lord, we prophesied in your name and cast out demons in your name and performed many miracles in your name." But I will reply, "I never knew you. Go away; the things you did were unauthorized."
>
> —MATTHEW 7:21–24

GOD'S WORD PRODUCES FRUIT

> The land produced vegetation: plants bearing seed according to their kinds and trees bearing fruit with seed in it according to their kinds. And God saw that it was good.
>
> —GENESIS 1:12, NIV

When the seed of the Word of God is planted in our heart it produces from the spirit love, joy, peace, patience, kindness, goodness, faithfulness, gentleness, and self-control.

The Word of God is the seed we must use against the adversary when we experience difficulties in our lives. This is one of the many reasons why one should want to seek God. It is very unfortunate that He only gets our attention during those painful experiences, when we have no place else to turn.

What kind of Word of God seed have you planted in your heart?

+ Some hear the message of the Word and allow the devil to steal it from their hearts and prevent them from believing and being saved.

+ Some hear the messages and receive it with joy. However, they are not committed, so they believe for a while, then fall away when faced with temptation.

+ Some hear the message, and it is quickly drowned out by the cares, riches, and pleasures of life, so they never develop.

- Finally, the seed that falls on the good soil represents those Christians who hear God's Word and cling to it patiently to produce a huge harvest that is displayed in their lives. (See Luke 8:11–15.)

I realized after reading the Bible that although I knew of God and attended weekly services I never accepted Jesus Christ as my Lord and Savior. The reason for this was because I adhered to erroneous teachings, and I did not take responsibility for educating myself on the Word of God. I would have been doomed for eternal damnation had I continued to remain complacent concerning the Word of God. Fortunately, I realized the danger I faced had I not let God into my heart. It became extremely important for me not only to accept Jesus as my Lord and Savior but to share this important, life-changing message of light and truth with those who are wise enough to listen, receive, believe, and then do it.

One of the reasons I believe most Christians have a difficult time getting the message of the kingdom of God is that we are in a world where many are seeking instant gratification. Many are influenced by their surroundings. The things of the spirit work inversely to Earth's system. Under the kingdom of God we study, meditate, and speak the Word, and it develops faith, belief, and trust; then the desire comes into being. In the Earth's realm, we see, want, and acquire by any means necessary. The only way we will ever get a revelation of this principle of the kingdom of God is to spend time in the Word. The time spent in the Word will ultimately lead to an intimate, personal relationship with our heavenly Father.

Once I prayed and asked God for revelation, I continued to read the Scriptures, was receptive, and listened. He commenced to provide discernment a little at a time. God releases insight into His Word as we develop. It is the same process as the development of an infant. When a child is first born, dependency is completely on the parent or other care provider. Gradually, after years of learning, they are given more responsibility and ultimately become independent. Ultimately, if we have done our jobs according to the guide provided, the true source of wisdom will be the result. The same way our children depend on us for all provisions is the manner in which our heavenly Father wants us to call on Him for every need. God is our true Source and will meet every need. Directions come to us from the promptings of our inner spirit when we listen.

Many will have a very difficult time with this. Why? Our sense of intellect will keep us from getting it. Like it or not, although our Creator has given us free will, He has the final authority. Would it not make sense to submit to the Guidebook that leads to peaceful journey?

THE BODY OF CHRIST

The body of Christ is the life of Jesus to be lived by all believers. In this life, Jesus is the Firstborn, the Head, and believers are His body. The resurrection life of Jesus within believers is what makes the connection to His body. Are you certain that you are saved by the grace of God and a part of the body? Church attendance does not equate to salvation. The church is comprised of all believers worldwide and has nothing to do with religious affiliations.

> There is no longer Jew or Gentile, slave or free, male or female. For you are all Christians—you are one in Christ Jesus. And now that you belong to Christ, you are the true children of Abraham. You are his heirs, and now all the promises God gave to him belong to you.
> —GALATIANS 3:28–29)

The church building houses the church.

> Now I say to you that you are Peter, and upon this rock I will build my church, and all the powers of hell will not conquer it.
> —MATTHEW 16:18

God does not reside in manmade temples. He dwells within the believer (Acts 7:48). The building is not the church; instead, it is the place church meets. Believers do not go to church; they are it. As believers, we are owners of the most precious commodity in the Earth's realm. We have the record of the living revelation of the Creator of the universe within us. He is within His followers and offers us eternal security with salvation. He guarantees that once we receive salvation we will never lose it. It cannot get any better than that. As believers, we all should become familiar with the Bible before joining a local fellowship. We need to be firm in our beliefs in order to avoid being misled. Scripture warns of false doctrine:

> But there were also false prophets in Israel, just as there will be false teachers among you. They will cleverly teach destructive

heresies and even deny the Master who bought them. Theirs will
be a swift and terrible end.

—2 Peter 2:1

We need to be able to discern truth from error before becoming involved.
Are you able to explain why you believe? When we spend time in any church
building and do not get development from God's Word, our time is poorly
invested. There are churches whose main objective is to add members, but
spreading the gospel should be the true target. We are God's ambassadors.
Our function is to allow Him to do His work through us rather than spend
time creating our own work. There is no greater work in this life, on this
earth, than to be used as a vessel of reconciliation in the lives of lost people,
thereby affecting change in someone's entire destiny (Gal. 2:7).

We call ourselves Christians, but do we truly know Jesus? As followers, it
is extremely important that we understand His divinity.

> For in Christ the fullness of God lives in a human body, and you
> are complete through your union with Christ. He is the Lord over
> every ruler and authority in the universe.
>
> —Colossians 2:9–10

Scripture tells us that Jesus asked His disciples: "'Who do people say
that the Son of Man is?' 'Well,' they replied, 'some say John the Baptist,
some say Elijah, and others say Jeremiah or one of the other prophets.' Then
he asked them, 'Who do you say I am?' Simon Peter answered, 'You are the
Messiah, the Son of the living God'" (Matt. 16:13–16). This response came
to him from revelation of the Spirit of God. The Spirit of God provides
believers with discernment in the same manner as He did Simon Peter.

How do we discover who Jesus is? We start by becoming familiar with
the precepts in the Guidebook. Our Creator provided us with instructions
for daily living in the Earth's realm. It behooves all of us to know and use
them. It is impossible to know God without knowing the person of Jesus. It
is important to note that if we accept God's Word, Jesus is included in the
package. Both God and Jesus are woven together, and we cannot accept one
without the other. Jesus Christ is the great I am. Apart from Him, we will
never know God. Once believers receive this revelation, it will renew minds,
transform character, and create a yearning to pass on the gospel and impact
entire belief systems. A revelation of this enormity presides over where we
will spend eternity.

Many of us in the body of Christ do not understand the reason for the

Cross of Jesus Christ. Jesus was the Lamb of God that came to Earth to save humanity from sin. He became the Lamb of God so that humanity might become the child of God. This event was the greatest expression of God's love for humanity. Why did Jesus come? Jesus came into the world to set the captives free. He said, "And you will know the truth, and the truth will set you free" (John 8:32). He came to fulfill the Law, redeem mankind from its sinful nature, reveal the true nature of God to man, testify to the truth of the gospel, and to seek and save all that were lost in order to create fullness within the follower.

> Because of this, God raised him up to the heights of heaven and gave him a name that is above every other name, so that at the name of Jesus every knee will bow, in heaven and on earth and under the earth, and every tongue will confess that Jesus Christ is Lord, to the glory of God the Father.
> —PHILIPPIANS 2:9–11

From humanity's perception, nothing good could have come from the crucifixion of Jesus. However, as heartbreaking as it was, it is the most extraordinary act that God has done for the human race. His promises are stored up for those who believe in Him, in the crucifixion, and in the ultimate resurrection of Jesus Christ. Jesus was birthed into a world that He created. He was God and man simultaneously.

> Christ is the visible image of the invisible God. He existed before God made anything at all and is supreme over all creation. Christ is the one through whom God created everything in heaven and earth. He made the things we can see and the things we can't see— kings, kingdoms, rulers, and authorities. Everything has been created through him and for him. He existed before everything else began, and he holds all creation together. Christ is the head of the church, which is his body. He is the first of all who will rise from the dead, so he is first in everything. For God in all his fullness was pleased to live in Christ
> —COLOSSIANS 1:15–19

Jesus did not begin at His birth but instead pre-existed with God the Father in the heavenly realm. Jesus came to Earth by way of a miraculous conception through a virgin. He was born in Bethlehem and reared in Nazareth. There was a long period of silence in the life of Jesus, for prior to age twelve we hardly hear anything about Him in the Scriptures. All of a sudden we hear that his parents lost sight of Him while at the Passover celebration. He was discovered in the temple with the Pharisees having a theological discussion and told His parents He was about His Father's business. Jesus walked the Earth in human flesh like man; however, at no time did He ever cease to be God.

Out of nowhere John the Baptist appeared in the wilderness. Scripture says John preached the kingdom of God and the need for repentance from sin. People came from all over to repent of their sins and be baptized. Suddenly, in the midst of baptismal service, John pointed and said, "Look, there is the Lamb of God who takes sin away." He pointed to Jesus! When Jesus came to John to be baptized, John attempted to deter Him, saying "I need to be baptized by you." However, John conceded in obedience and to fulfill the will of the Father. When John performed the ceremony of baptism, the Spirit of the Lord came upon Jesus, anointing Him for the work He was sent out to do.

> And a voice from heaven said, "This is my beloved Son, and I am fully pleased with him."
> —MATTHEW 3:17

Shortly after this, Jesus retreated into the wilderness to fast, pray, and talk to the Father. Perhaps this retreat was to obtain some additional insight for the assignment He came to do. How would He move into the world to launch His ministry? During these forty days in the wilderness Satan tempted Him and tried to divert Him with many enticements. However, Jesus always came back at Him with the Word. Eventually Satan realized His defeat, and Jesus surfaced from the wilderness preaching the kingdom of heaven. When He preached, many gathered to listen. There was something miraculous about the authority in which He spoke.

Jesus Christ is the most valuable gift ever given to humanity. He is the Alpha and the Omega, the Light of the world, and the Bread of life. He is our teacher, counselor, helper, truth, and the vow guaranteeing redemption and eternal life. As believers it is important that we are able to articulate this truth to the nonbelieving world.

Just as Jesus used the Word to defeat Satan, believers have been given the same authority to use it in their daily lives. In the absence of the knowledge of God's Word, believers become followers of the world's wicked ways. We are the leaders of the world, so it is crucial take on the charge in a proactive manner.

It is very difficult to bring unbelievers into churches because our behavior is not aligned with true Christian principles and does not reflect full adherence to the Word of God. Therefore, there is no incentive to join. No one should need to ask whether or not we are Christians. Our actions should reflect it. God intended for the church to be based in His agenda, not the agenda of saints. It was not intended to be a country club, a social gathering place, or a branch of corporate America. It should be a place of worship, praise, and fellowship to and for God. Our guidelines should come from prayer and Holy Spirit revelation, not from personal objectives.

> Above all, you must understand that no prophecy in Scripture ever came from the prophets themselves or because they wanted to prophesy. It was the Holy Spirit who moved the prophets to speak from God.
> —2 PETER 1:20–21

The first thing I had to do when I made the commitment to pursue God was to find a church. My goal was to find one that operated under biblical principles and was based on the Word of God. I grew up in the Roman Catholic Church, and that was no longer an option for me. While practicing in the Catholic faith, I had not experienced the teaching of true biblical principles. Service was basically a ritual more than anything else. In hindsight, like many, attending church was mainly to help me feel better about myself, not to gain biblical insight. Based on my experience, the leadership of the Roman Catholic Church created dependency rather than development.

In June 2012, my sister was in the hospital. On Sunday morning she attended a Roman Catholic mass, and when she went up to receive communion she was told no. They told her that since she had not confessed to the priest prior, she could not receive communion. I believe that someone forgot to educate the leaders in the Roman Catholic Church that Jesus came and set the captives free. Therefore, we no longer need an intermediary to whom we must confess our sins. We were redeemed by the blood of Jesus when we accepted Him as Lord and Savior. We need do nothing but receive His grace, as we have been given authority to go directly to God in the name of Jesus and confess our sins. The priest does not have the authority to block the sacrament from anyone. In fact, the priest has no more authority than any other believer. Divine authority supersedes any other, including that of the hierarchy of the Roman Catholic Church. When my sister told the priest the veil had been lifted, he was stunned and did not know what to say to her. She walked away from the service.

We continue with rituals because of ignorance to the laws of the kingdom of God. If we continue to remain complacent to the laws that God has so freely placed in our hands, we will remain useless to serve according to His will. The way we serve will be derived from our own self-serving agendas, not His plan. This is another example of the dependency the Roman Catholic Church creates among the saints.

Several years ago I had the opportunity to listen to an interview. The conversation was about the passing of a prominent political and world figure. The son of leader referenced said the following: "My father's major cause of anguish was that he was not sure if the Pope forgave his sins." When I heard that statement, I was shocked. I said to myself, here is a member of our society who was well educated, a political leader, and labeled as a role model citizen, whom many emulated. However, He spent an entire lifetime in the earthly realm without knowing what his true purpose in life was. Think about this, What was his real accomplishment? Was it the money he left for his family? Was it the number of times he was elected to office? Was it the laws that got passed while in office? You decide! We are here in the Earth's realm for God's purpose. When we are working on causes that are not aligned with His will for humanity, we are self-serving.

This revelation was not a surprise. It was just a reminder that teachings in the Roman Catholic Church remain the same. I say this humbly and without malice nor disrespect to the hierarchy of the Catholic Church: All believers in Jesus Christ have equal authority and power as any leader in any church. Our Father, God almighty, Lord, Creator of the universe, and King of kings, has given us full authority to go directly to Him in the name of Jesus. Do not put your spiritual illumination in the hands of any leader. God gave us the Guidebook, and He will hold us accountable. Both believers and non-believers are accountable to God. Scripture tells us, "As surely as I live,' says the Lord, every knee will bow to me and every tongue will confess allegiance to God" (Rom. 14:11). There is no excuse for us to be in ignorance to the Word of God, unless we are in a remote part of the world with no access to it.

Step Up From Complacency

God intended for us believers to be a cut above others in the world so that He might use us to lure unbelievers into His kingdom. We are not useful for the kingdom without knowledge of the Word. Faith will not work until the will of God is known. You might ask, What is the will of God? God's Word is His will for all humanity. If we truly understood who we are in Jesus and what Christ has done for us, we would all be living from an intimate union, following direction from the Holy Spirit instead of being entangled by religious traditions.

Many believe that going to the church building on Sundays means that they are in the kingdom of God. But following Christ means more than going to church. In the life of Jesus there was no rush for endless activities. Likewise, we should rid ourselves of the spirit of religion and strive to develop an intimate, personal relationship with Jesus. God set up the universe with very definite spiritual laws. Until we choose to make them final authority in our lives, He is unable to use us to accomplish His will for others here on Earth.

To seek God is to read His Word, not sometimes or once in a while when we have time, but daily. Only then can we begin to receive discernment of the plan He has for our lives. We waste precious time when we do not know our Creator's will for our lives. I know this because I wasted a lot of years in ignorance to the Word. Divine discernment of this assignment only came after an incessant pursuit of God. At that point it became clear that He is always available to us, just as He declared in His Word: "I am with you always, even to the end of the age" (Matt. 28:20). We need to pursue Him in the same manner we pursue other interest.

When we turn to God and believe and accept what He reveals in the Word, the miraculous atonement of the cross of Christ instantly places us in a right relationship with the Almighty. All of God's servants on assignment were ordinary people who were able to accomplish the extraordinary in His strength. We have no idea how, when, or where God is going to engineer future circumstances. With no knowledge of the adversities that will come forth, it is prudent to be prepared with the resource of the Word of God. His Word will undoubtedly provide a peace that surpasses all understanding during those periods: "Peace I leave with you; my peace I give you. I do not give to you as the world gives. Do not let your hearts be troubled and do not be afraid" (John 14:27, NIV). We are so slow to learn the lessons God wants to teach us that by the time we get it, we have missed quite a bit of His blessings. However, better late than to die and not know His awesome truth.

God will be persistent with us. The Israelites had been taken into captivity because of their sin, but the same problems arose again because, just like us, they did not get it. The people were neglecting worship, prayer, and the teachings of God's Word. Not to mention, they were treating each other unjustly. They were unloving and unforgiving. However, in His patience, God continued to send His messengers to them to offer direction.

If we obey kingdom laws, we have superseded all of the earthly ones. Therefore, we will not focus on ungodly practices. A personal relationship with the Creator of the universe provides us with access to an arsenal of tools to be used against the adversary during our times of struggle. The kingdom of God's constitution (the Bible) creates fear among many. These people rely on a pastor, priest, rabbi, or teacher not only to deliver the message but to also be the source of all biblical enlightenment, which was not our Creator's intent. God has a personal message for each and every one of us. However, we will not get it without time spent in the Word. It is the single tool required to start a personal, intimate relationship with Him.

Think for a moment. What kind of relationship would you have with your husband, wife, children or friends, if you only spent a couple of hours a week with them and never spent time to speak to them or learn more about them? The same applies to God. We cannot learn His ways with a once- or twice-a-week message. If we do not read the Bible, we will never understand what to expect when we are confronted with difficulties. Adversities are unavoidable; they are a part of the journey. However, when we are knowledgeable about our resources, we are likely to lean on the Holy Spirit to help us make godly choices.

As difficult as this might be to the average believer who has experienced life difficulties, it is during these trials that we are given the opportunity to get in the Word of God and gain insight, revelation, and wisdom from above. When Jesus went to the cross He said, "It is finished!" (John 19:30). This meant that He took all our pain, sickness, lack, and gave us His grace. We were all released from bondage. It continues to be mind boggling how we just cannot get it.

To become physically fit, we must exercise, set an agenda, or begin a regimen. The same applies to our spiritual growth. Spiritual strength requires equal work as physical training. Before an athlete runs a marathon, he needs to prepare. Likewise, to combat difficulties we are confronted with on a daily basis, we need to be equipped with the Word of God. Thus far, the Bible is the only fail-proof resource in existence in the Earth's realm. To become spiritually powerful we need to apply resistance. How is this accomplished? Well, we know that faith comes by hearing, and hearing by the Word of God. We further know from the Bible that "the word of God is full of living power. It is sharper than the sharpest knife, cutting into our innermost thoughts and desires. It exposes us for what we really are" (Heb. 4:12). Study the Bible and learn how to apply the power of the Word of the living God to your burdens.

Greatness in God requires a change in our thought pattern. He has promised to get us through any and all difficulties. The key is to turn all the cares over to Him. Knowledge of the Word, coupled with obedience, trust, and faith is the key to victory in the kingdom of God. Here is what God said in His Word about the role He plays in our lives:

> Give your burdens to the LORD, and he will take care of you. He will not permit the godly to slip and fall.
> —PSALM 55:22

The body of Christ is coming up short. Believers have failed to recognize the will of God in their lives because they are not reading the Book. The responsibility of reading and meditating on God's Word is that of the believer. Final judgment will not be a family, team, group, or national effort; it will be an individual one. Here is a suggested action plan:

Carve out a plan to spend time with the Lord daily, and commit to it. Treat this as the most important assignment of your life. I assure you that when you make God the final authority in your life, you will begin to experience a true taste of the supernatural and extraordinary.

WE ARE THE TEMPLE OF GOD

In the old covenant, God had a temple for His people. Today in the new covenant, God placed His temple in our heart. We are able to say this because we have been redeemed by the death of Jesus, and the Holy Spirit now has taken residence within us.

> Don't you realize that all of you together are the temple of God and that the Spirit of God lives in you?
> —1 CORINTHIANS 3:16

I do not believe that many of us are aware that our bodies are the temple of God. What does this mean? We should be the ones to lead by example in our love toward each other. What we do with our body and what we put in it matters to God. As temporary owners of this earthly tent we live in, we have the responsibility to honor our Creator by honoring it. How? We must read the Guidebook and follow the rules. Do not be deceived with the world's view of living. God's Word provides divine wisdom for the upkeep of our earthly tent.

> And so, dear brothers and sisters, I plead with you to give your bodies to God. Let them be a living and holy sacrifice—the kind

he will accept. When you think of what he has done for you, is this too much to ask? Don't copy the behavior and customs of this world, but let God transform you into a new person by changing the way you think. Then you will know what God wants you to do, and you will know how good and pleasing and perfect his will really is.

　　　　　　　　　　　　　　　　　　　　—ROMANS 12:1–2

As the Scriptures state, "Stop fooling yourselves. If you think you are wise by this world's standards, you will have to become a fool so you can become wise by God's standards. For the wisdom of this world is foolishness to God. As the Scriptures say, 'God catches those who think they are wise in their own cleverness.' And again, 'The Lord knows the thoughts of the wise, that they are worthless.' So don't take pride in following a particular leader. Everything belongs to you: Paul and Apollos and Peter; the whole world and life and death; the present and the future. Everything belongs to you, and you belong to Christ, and Christ belongs to God" (1 Cor. 3:18–23).

When we recognize what has been given to us in Christ, it's a cause for real celebration. Every believer has the Holy Spirit, a living Spirit Being, one of the three members of the Godhead, living within us: "Don't you know that your body is the temple of the Holy Spirit, who lives in you and was given to you by God? You do not belong to yourself" (1 Cor. 6:19). This provides us with spiritual freedom where we trust the Word to do what God says it will do.

> From eternity to eternity I am God. No one can oppose what I do.
> No one can reverse my actions.
> 　　　　　　　　　　　　　　　　　　　　—ISAIAH 43:13

True freedom means living without the burden that sin creates. Jesus Christ paid the price; therefore, we are free from the lure of the devil. Any behavior that violates the human body is not permissible for followers of Jesus Christ.

> Don't team up with those who are unbelievers. How can goodness be a partner with wickedness? How can light live with darkness? What harmony can there be between Christ and the Devil ? How can a believer be a partner with an unbeliever? And what union can there be between God's temple and idols? For we are the temple of the living God. As God said: "I will live in them and walk among them. I will be their God, and they will be my people. Therefore,

come out from them and separate yourselves from them, says the
Lord. Don't touch their filthy things, and I will welcome you. And
I will be your Father, and you will be my sons and daughters, says
the Lord Almighty."

—2 CORINTHIANS 6:14–18

HUMAN SOLUTIONS TO PERILS

When we know God's Word we never look to human solutions to our problems. Why? God is the only source of omniscience. Therefore, it would be
unwise to seek any guidance other than the One who knows the beginning,
middle, and ending. The Word of God creates what mere man will never
get from logic. God intended for us to be conformed to kingdom culture.
However, the opposite has occurred, and when things go wrong God always
gets the blame. Instead, we need to place blame on our rebellion for many of
our struggles.

My people are destroyed from lack of knowledge.

—HOSEA 4:6, NIV

What do you believe God is referring to? It is the Bible. Think of the
scenarios people write in books daily. They write about subjects that are
supposedly important to us, and we derive great value from them. However,
none would ever provide the wisdom our Creator has already made available to us. We purchase gadgets and read the owner's manuals to ensure
we use them correctly, yet we don't consult the user's manual for our own
lives. It is amazing that we have such a difficult time accepting guidance
from the One who created all things. We choose to settle for ordinary in
lieu of the supernaturally extraordinary. Human's power is short-lived and
very temporal. We might believe we are powerful because of wealth, careers,
education, and social position; however, in the end, those things are all
meaningless to God. Real power only comes from the Spirit of God within
those who believe in Jesus Christ. God's Word applied to our lives is truly
the power.

And I have given you authority over all the power of the enemy,
and you can walk among snakes and scorpions and crush them.
Nothing will injure you.

—LUKE 10:19

PART 2:
RELATIONSHIPS AND SURROUNDINGS MATTER

Pay Attention

ORDER YOUR STEPS

IN THIS CHAPTER I have been led by the Spirit of God to discuss the way in which Christians occupy themselves in religious activities to fulfill spiritual obligations rather than truly developing a relationship with God. There is a major difference between religion and relationship. The definition of *religion* found at *Dictionary.com* is "the body of persons adhering to a particular set of beliefs and practices…ritual observances of faith."[1] It defines *intimacy* as "a close familiar, and usually affectionate or loving personal relationship with another person or group."[2] Religion does not provide for communion with our Creator. Predominantly, what it does is keep us burdened with rituals that have nothing to do with our personal relationship with God.

I am sharing information, not promulgating a law to change any individual's belief system. However, rituals have kept many in regression, unable to connect with the Spirit of God within the believer. In the absence of an intimate, personal relationship with our Creator, His message will elude us. Therefore, it is important that we order our steps so that we might accomplish the mandate. Although religious activities play a role in our spiritual development, our heavenly Father is not interested in self-serving religious activities. Instead, He is interested in a personal, intimate relationship with each believer in the body of Christ. One of the most assured ways to order our steps is to "seek ye first the kingdom of God, and his righteousness; and all these things shall be added to you" (Matt. 6:33, KJV).

Many of us in the body of Christ have fallen into complacency. How? We have been given access to God by way of the Cross; however, we have failed to connect with Him and depend on the promptings of the Holy Spirit. Instead, we are making decisions that are completely disconnected from the Spirit of God within the believer. God requires those of us who make up the body of Christ to be a cut above the rest of the world. We are the salt of the Earth, the leaders of the world. However, many of us have not lived up to this standard and have succumbed to the flesh by becoming followers of worldly ways. In adherence to our role of discipleship, we are called to lead the next generation of young people in the truth and light of God. Until we embrace the guidance of the Word of God, God's positioning system (GPS), we will continue to be followers and lead the next generations into a continued ignorance of God.

In order to understand access to the gateway into the kingdom of God, we must comprehend Christ's agony in the Garden of Gethsemane. This was the garden where the most famous event occurred on the night before Jesus' crucifixion. After Jesus and His disciples had celebrated the Passover, they came to the garden. After this, Judas Iscariot, the betrayer, arrived with a multitude of soldiers, the high priest, Pharisees, and servants to arrest Jesus. Judas identified Him by the prearranged signal of a kiss, which he gave to Jesus. (See John 18.)

Jesus' anguish was getting through the work as the Son of Man. He knew that it could be done as the Son of God. Jesus' assignment was to redeem humanity from its sinful nature by way of the cross, and Satan could not overpower Him in the realm of the spirit. The suffering at Gethsemane was the Son of God's to fulfill, His destiny as Savior of humanity. When we understand this, it becomes possible for us to value the importance of the relationship. The entire human race has been provided access into God's presence because of the Cross. Why should we order our steps? One day we will give an account of ourselves to the Lord, and we must order the passageway with the steps to get there successfully.

+ Clear your cluttered minds. Allow God to guide you by way of the Holy Spirit within.

+ Make time for God daily. Begin each day by reading God's Word.

Wise words satisfy like a good meal.
—PROVERBS 18:20

Yes, each of us will have to give a personal account to God. So don't condemn each other anymore. Decide instead to live in such a way that you will not put an obstacle in another Christian's path.
—ROMANS 14:12

There are many areas in which we require knowledge and understanding so that we might accomplish our individual mandate from the kingdom. Follow the guidance of the Word, become acquainted with the steps, and receive benefits while still in Earth's realm.

We were all created to be of service to the Creator of the universe. However, many in the body of Christ are not in compliance. Why? Because our unawareness of the kingdom laws and our practice of self-serving behavior distract us from the objective. The more tumultuous the life the easier it is to say, "Look out for number one." Are you living for yourself? We all have a multitude of responsibilities clamoring for our attention. Some are very important, while others are not so essential. However, none will ever offer the spiritual richness and roundedness that is put forward in the light of God. If we allow the truth of Scripture to renew our mind and turn away from ideas and behaviors that thwart our thoughts and spoken words, God will richly reward us.

Many have given their life to Christ and are sitting in the pews of churches weekly; however, acceptance of Jesus Christ as Lord and Savior and attending church are only the first steps. There is so much more to developing a relationship with God. I grew up in the Roman Catholic Church and was never introduced to the message of salvation. I am uncertain as to why I missed that teaching. Perhaps it was because reading and studying the Bible were not part of my daily regimen. However, I blame myself for not taking responsibility for my spiritual development. As a result of my inaction as it relates to my relationship with God, I was not saved and, until ten years ago, operated in ignorance. Salvation came for me when I seriously pursued God. When I realized that salvation is the key to enter into the kingdom of God, I made it my business to learn the steps. I immersed myself in the Word twenty-four seven for ten years and still continue to do so. For most, immersing oneself this deeply is likely unreasonable. However, you can follow your heart to determine what level of commitment works for you. I treat the Word of God the same as food and make time for the Word of God daily.

> I have not departed from the commands of his lips; I have treasured the words of mouth more than my daily bread.
> —Job 23:12, niv

I do not allow anything to take priority over the time I spend in communion with our Creator. For me, it is a lifestyle and a commitment. In the same way that our bodies require food daily to remain healthy, the Word is the food we need for spiritual sustenance. Without the Word we have a tendency to allow our flesh to rule, rather than our spirit.

It is very unfortunate that the Bible only became my light after a visit with the school of hard knocks, also known as the perils of life. According to a 2007 Gallup News Service poll conducted by Princeton University, only 23 percent of Christians who attend church regularly have spiritual growth and guidance as their objective.[3] Perhaps this accounts for why the Bible is not a tool used in the lives of many Christians.

In the remaining sections of this chapter, I will share some of the teachings and important steps I learned that are required to live in the light of God.

STEP 1: KNOW THE ORIGIN OF YOUR FREEDOM

Freedom in Christ

A person is never really free unless they are free on the inside. Many people say and believe that they are free. However, they are completely unaware of their oppression. Some of the world's most affluent people are living in bondage, yet they have no idea of it. Jesus Christ is the only one with the ability and authority to really set us free. Why were we set free? God's love for humanity! How did He set us free? Jesus took the sin of all of humanity when He died on the cross.

> So Christ has really set us free. Now make sure that you stay free,
> and don't get tied up again in slavery to the law.
> —GALATIANS 5:1

No human has ever endured or is equipped to bear all the sin of mankind. The blood of Jesus gave us redemption. He bore the pain for all sickness, lack, and poverty for the entire human race. There is no need for us to revisit those maladies because He has already done so. So why is humanity in bondage to sin? It is because of our ignorance to the gift Jesus gave to humanity. Think about this: If a friend paid off your mortgage, would you continue making payments to the bank? No, odds are you would receive the blessing and save your money or use it for something else important to you. The same applies here. When we know the Word, we do the Word.

If at any time we fall back into sin, we need only go to the Father immediately and repent. God loves humanity so much that He allows never ending grace when we sin. This does not mean we have a license to continually to sin. What it does mean is that God forgives us if we truly repent from our heart. Likewise, we should forgive others. God continuously forgives us; however, we have the audacity to be unforgiving to our fellow humans. If we have a relationship with God, forgiveness should be in our hearts.

With knowledge and understanding, we take all that Jesus already provided through the Cross and the blood. The Word of God carries the authority and power to produce the entire requirement to live life successfully in the Earth's realm. If we let the truth of Scripture fill our mind, guard our emotions, and influence our conduct, God will richly reward us with spiritual blessings.

> So now there is no condemnation for those who belong to Christ Jesus. For the power of the life-giving Spirit has freed you through Christ Jesus from the power of sin that leads to death. The law of Moses could not save us, because of our sinful nature. But God put into effect a different plan to save us. He sent his own Son in a human body like ours, except that ours are sinful. God destroyed sin's control over us by giving his Son as a sacrifice for our sins. He did this so that the requirement of the law would be fully accomplished for us who no longer follow our sinful nature but instead follow the Spirit. Those who are dominated by the sinful nature think about sinful things, but those who are controlled by the Holy Spirit think about things that please the Spirit. If your sinful nature controls your mind, there is death. But if the Holy Spirit controls your mind, there is life and peace. For the sinful nature is always hostile to God. It never did obey God's laws, and it never will. That's why those who are still under the control of their sinful nature can never please God.
> —ROMANS 8:1–8

Order your steps to the light of God. In the absence of a relationship with the Creator of the universe, true freedom is unattainable.

STEP 2: EXTRAORDINARY NEWS

Good News for the Oppressed

> The thief's purpose is to steal and kill and destroy. My purpose is to give life in all its fullness.
> —JOHN 10:10

To *oppress* is "to burden, with cruel or unjust impositions or restraints; subject to harsh exercise of authority or power."[4] Are you oppressed? Many might not consider themselves oppressed because they have what they perceive to be success based on financial status. Being oppressed, according to the flesh, is a label that is usually attached to the downtrodden. Unfortunately, that is not an accurate depiction of the oppressed according to the kingdom. If we find ourselves in ignorance to the kingdom of God and its laws, we have fallen into oppression.

The Spirit of the Sovereign LORD is upon me, because the LORD has appointed me to bring good news to the poor. He has sent me to comfort the brokenhearted and to announce that captives will be released and prisoners will be freed. He has sent me to tell those who mourn that the time of the LORD's favor has come, and with it, the day of God's anger against their enemies.

—ISAIAH 61:1–2

What is this good news? The good news of Jesus Christ is the gospel message that Jesus did what mere man was unable to do. He died as a substitute in our place to make atonement for our sins and put all who believe in God into a right relationship with Him. His resurrection was the stamp of approval of all He did on the hill of Calvary on the cross.

STEP 3: BELIEVE YOU ARE THE LIGHT OF THE WORLD

Jesus is the light of the world, and our acceptance of Him made believers also luminous. He left and gave us a commission to preach the Word throughout the world. He gave humanity authority over all things in the Earth's realm. How do we release this authority? Acceptance of Him as Lord and Savior, coupled with faith.

Godly confidence is based on:

+ Our position in Christ: It is discovered as we read God's Word.

+ Our perspective of Christ: It develops as we grow in the relationship.

+ The promises of Christ.

Christ's promises include:

1. To be with us

And we can be confident that he will listen to us whenever we ask him for anything in line with his will.

—1 JOHN 5:14

2. To provide for us

And this same God who takes care of me will supply all your needs from his glorious riches, which have been given to us in Christ Jesus.

—PHILIPPIANS 4:19

3. To empower us

For you did not receive a spirit that makes you a slave again to fear, but you received the Spirit of sonship. And by him we cry, "'Abba,' Father."

—ROMANS 8:15, NIV

4. To strengthen us

Don't be afraid, for I am with you. Do not be dismayed, for I am your God. I will strengthen you. I will help you. I will uphold you with my victorious right hand.

—ISAIAH 41:10

God chose Israel to be a model nation that would encourage other nations to want to come under His rule (Exod. 19:3–8). Even with knowledge of God's laws, man still needs the Holy Spirit to live the life He preordained for humanity.

I see very clearly that God doesn't show partiality.

—ACTS 10:34

STEP 4: KNOW YOU ARE CHOSEN

We Are All Chosen

God chose you.

You didn't choose me. I chose you. I appointed you to go and produce fruit that will last, so that the Father will give you whatever you ask for, using my name.

—JOHN 15:16

We are all chosen! Are you listening? The Lord chose disciples and sent them in pairs to all the towns and villages He planned to visit. Did you know that as a believer, you are one of God's disciples? These are perilous times, and He needs for every believer to spread the good news.

These were His instructions to them:

The harvest is great, but the workers are so few. Pray to the Lord who is in charge of the harvest, and ask him to send out workers for his fields. Go now, and remember that I am sending you out as lambs among wolves…Whenever you enter a home, give it your blessing. If those who live there are worthy, the blessing will stand; if

they are not, the blessing will return to you. When you enter a town,
don't move around from home to home. Stay in one place, eating and
drinking what they provide you. Don't hesitate to accept hospitality,
because those who work deserve their pay.

—LUKE 10:2–3, 5–7

How do we as believers help to accomplish this mandate from our heavenly Father? Simple! We imitate God the way our children imitate us. We
become doers of His Word and follow the direction given in the Guidebook
for life. We do what the Word says we should do. We become imitators of
God's Word instead of becoming followers of the ignorant and rebellious
ways of the world. Choose well.

STEP 5: CHOOSE FAITH OVER FEAR

Our heavenly Father is interested in every area of our lives. When we choose
to be fearful, it hinders us from becoming the people God wants us to be.
Think about this. God gave the Holy Spirit to every believer as a Helper.
Therefore, He provided all the required elements that enable faithful living.
Our responsibility is to partake of the spiritual Word of God food in the
Bible. God guides us for His pleasure and our benefit. Only with reading
the Word of God daily are we able to follow the Holy Spirit's guidance.

> Let nothing be done through selfish ambition or conceit, but in
> lowliness of mind let each esteem others better than himself. Let
> each of you look out not only for his own interests, but also for the
> interests of others.
>
> —PHILIPPIANS 2:3–4, NKJV

The new life in salvation needs to emulate the newly discovered Jesus
within.

> For God is working in you, giving you the desire to obey him and
> the power to do what pleases him.
>
> —PHILIPPIANS 2:13

Because of Adam and Eve's disobedience to God's command in the
garden, the Lord instituted a new covenant in order to release humanity
from the position of sin.

> Once you were dead, doomed forever because of your many sins. You
> used to live just like the rest of the world, full of sin, obeying Satan,

the mighty prince of the power of the air. He is the spirit at work in the hearts of those who refuse to obey God. All of us used to live that way, following the passions and desires of our evil nature. We were born with an evil nature, and we were under God's anger just like everyone else. But God is so rich in mercy, and he loved us so very much, that even while we were dead because of our sins, he gave us life when he raised Christ from the dead. (It is only by God's special favor that you have been saved!) For he raised us from the dead along with Christ, and we are seated with him in the heavenly realms—all because we are one with Christ Jesus.

—Ephesians 2:1–6

Remember, believers have been given a new life in Christ Jesus. Let us display that new life by being an obedient doer of God's Word instead of just a hearer.

Step 6: Be Obedient to the Word

Tithing

During these difficult economic times, most of us are thinking about our finances. However, do our financial plans match those prepared by our Creator? God's financial plans are birthed from the seed of His divine promise. Fortunately, God's financial plans supersede those plans in the Earth's realm. God, in His omniscience, did not omit anything. Therefore, when you trust God there is no need to worry about your finances. However, He has some basic commands for our finances, including taking care of the poor and tithing.

God talks about money in His Word and has made financial promises accordingly. It is important to note that all God's promises are subject to our free will. However, disobedience in any area of God's commands results in loss of blessings. God's financial plan clearly stipulates that we are to give a tenth of every dollar earned. All our earnings are essentially attributable to Him, so why begrudge the command? When we decide to make up our own laws regarding tithing and offering, we open the door to the adversary. We are basically saying, "I know what is best for my finances, so I will give what I want to give." What God does when we are obedient to the tithing mandate is unfailingly clear. We cannot out-give God. The more we give in service to the Lord, the more we will get from Him in return. This is the only area in the Bible where God says "test me" (Mal. 3:10, NIV). In Malachi, when the scriptures say, "Should people cheat God? Yet you have cheated me" (Mal. 3:8). God is saying to the believer, "You are bringing tithes and offerings to me. However, it is not a tenth of your earnings as outlined in Scripture. Hence you have cheated God."

> "Bring all the tithes into the storehouse so there will be enough food in my Temple. If you do," says the LORD Almighty, "I will open the windows of heaven for you. I will pour out a blessing so great you won't have enough room to take it in! Try it! Let me prove it to you!"
> —MALACHI 3:10

> He who refreshes others will himself be refreshed.
> —PROVERBS 11:25, NIV

> If you give, you will receive. Your gift will return to you in full measure, pressed down, shaken together to make room for more, and running over. Whatever measure you use in giving—large or small— it will be used to measure what is given back to you.
> —LUKE 6:38

What is the tithe?

The *tithe* is "the tenth part of agricultural produce or personal income set apart as an offering to God for works of mercy...or...for the support of the church."[5] The Bible records numerous accounts of man tithing to God. Abraham tithed to Melchizedek, Isaac tithed, and so did his son Jacob and many others way before the Law. God is the Creator of everything that exists. He owns everything, and we are simply stewards who have been entrusted with His blessings. God gives to us, and we give back one-tenth of all that He has blessed us with. The tithe was intended to get supernatural blessings to God's children.

Many Christians struggle with the issue of tithing, refusing to submit to the biblical exhortation about making offerings to the Lord. Tithing is intended to be a joy. Instead, in many churches it becomes drudgery. I know this from present experiences and conversations I have had with other Christians regarding tithing. For me personally, I believe that giving a tenth of my income back to God is demonstrating thankfulness to Him for what He has provided. It also helps me to remember that God is my Source. He does not need our finances; His purpose is to bless us. Giving should be out of reverence to God. If we give grudgingly, it is better if we do not give. Now that we have become a part of the kingdom of God, a most important step is to tithe. Why should we tithe? Out of faithfulness and honor to God. There is a great blessing that comes from obedience.

What happens when we fail to tithe? Although God has given us free will in every area of our lives, when we fail to tithe we rob Him. Covertness causes us to lose blessings. If we give God what belongs to Him, He will ensure that we get what belongs to us. Do you have peace in all areas of your life? My revelation on the tithing came to me as I immersed in the study of the Word. I believe many refuse to tithe because there is a lack of understanding regarding the principal of tithing. Why not take God at His Word and tithe? Test Him as His Word states and reap the benefits of giving.

An extended period of adversity will definitely open your mind and heart to consider this principle. I understood and trusted the Word of God to do as it said. Fortunately for me, the Word performed its work. How can we become cheerful givers? Emulate the steps of the greatest Giver of all times, Jesus. He came to Earth and willingly gave His life so that we might keep ours. There can be no better way to honor Jesus than by giving selflessly the way He did. Remember the words of the Lord Jesus:

> It is more blessed to give than to receive.
>
> —Acts 20:35

Continue to engage and never drift away.

> So we must listen very carefully to the truth we have heard, or we may drift away from it. The message God delivered through angels has always proved true, and the people were punished for every violation of the law and every act of disobedience. What makes us think that we can escape if we are indifferent to this great salvation that was announced by the Lord Jesus himself? It was passed on to us by those who heard him speak, and God verified the message by signs and wonders and various miracles and by giving gifts of the Holy Spirit whenever he chose to do so.
>
> —Hebrews 2:1–4

It will do us well to know that we are saved because God so generously gave. Every Christian should diligently pray and seek God's wisdom in the matter of tithing.

> If you need wisdom—if you want to know what God wants you to do—ask him, and he will gladly tell you. He will not resent your asking.
>
> —James 1:5

STEP 7: BE AWARE OF THE ADVERSARY

The Devil Deceives

Did you know that the devil knows God's Word? He certainly does, and in order for us to be alerted to his tricks we also need to know and fight back with God's Word. We can learn a great deal about this from reading the account of the temptation of Jesus:

> Then Jesus was led out into the wilderness by the Holy Spirit to be tempted there by the Devil. For forty days and forty nights he ate nothing and became very hungry. Then the Devil came and said to him, "If you are the Son of God, change these stones into loaves of bread." But Jesus told him, "No! The Scriptures say, 'People need more than bread for their life; they must feed on every word of God.'" Then the Devil took him to Jerusalem, to the highest point of the Temple, and said, "If you are the Son of God, jump off! For the Scriptures say, 'He orders his angels to protect you. And they will hold you with their hands to keep you from striking your foot on a stone.'" Jesus responded, "The Scriptures also say, 'Do not test the Lord your God.'" Next the Devil took him to the peak of a very high mountain and showed him the nations of the world and all their glory. "I will give it all to you," he said, "if you will only kneel down and worship me." "Get out of here, Satan," Jesus told him. "For the Scriptures say, 'You must worship the Lord your God; serve only him.'" Then the Devil went away, and angels came and cared for Jesus.
>
> —MATTHEW 4:1–11

What is to be expected when we accept offers from the devil? Eve was deceived by the devil because she believed that an independence from God would provide more freedom. What appeared to be an extraordinary deal in the Garden of Eden resulted in a life of sin and oppression handed down to humanity. What appeals to you? For many, money is the god. Many people have different things that appeal to them, and much of it is based on worldly desires. However, God has secrets that are way greater than money that He will only reveal to those who pursue Him.

> Then he explained to them, "You have been permitted to understand the secrets of the Kingdom of Heaven, but others have not. To those who are open to my teaching, more understanding will be given, and they will have an abundance of knowledge. But to those

who are not listening, even what they have will be taken away from them. That is why I tell these stories, because people see what I do, but they don't really see. They hear what I say, but they don't really hear, and they don't understand.

—MATTHEW 13:11–13

Jesus spoke in parables, which makes it difficult for outsiders to understand. With God, all blessings are provided freely. However, in order to partake of the kingdom of God's inheritance, we are required to abide by the laws. Mostly, we have not because we ask not. The story of the rich man who made the tragic choice of living for himself without regard to God is an example of how we allow money to cloud our perspective. (See Luke 18:18–25.) Jesus was asked by a rich man, "Good Teacher, what should I do to get eternal life?" (v. 18). Jesus said, "But as for your question, you know the commandments: 'Do not commit adultery. Do not murder. Do not steal. Do not testify falsely. Honor your father and mother.' The man replied, 'I've obeyed all these commandments since I was a child'" (vv. 20–21). When Jesus heard his answer, he said, "There is still one thing you lack…Sell all you have and give the money to the poor, and you will have treasures in heaven. Then come, follow me. But when the man heard this, he became very sad because he was very rich. Jesus watched him go and then said to the disciples, "How hard it is for rich people to get into the Kingdom of God! It is easier for a camel to go through the eye of a needle than for a rich person to enter the Kingdom of God!" (vv. 22–25). When the man heard this he became very sad, for he was very rich. The rich man had a mentality to hoard his wealth.

When we indulge in a relationship with the devil we are treading in dangerous territory. Liberty to be self-made is slavery to self and sin. The only way we are able to receive the freedom from bondage Jesus purchased for us is when we are protected by the boundaries of the kingdom of God. Order your steps to formulate godly objectives by using the Bible as a resource to accomplish God's intention.

Be strong and very courageous. Obey all the laws Moses gave you. Do not turn away from them, and you will be successful in everything you do. Study this Book of the Law continually. Meditate on it day and night so you may be sure to obey all that is written in it. Only then will you succeed. I command you—be strong and courageous! Do not be afraid or discouraged. For the Lord your God is with you wherever you go.

—JOSHUA 1:7–9

6
BE MINDFUL OF SURROUNDINGS

WHO IS IN your sphere of influence? Our sphere of influence determines our temporal or eternal success. Whoever we allow in our sphere dictates the level of light or darkness that comes into our lives. If we are surrounded with people who are in the light, our experience will be love, joy, and peace. Likewise, if we are surrounded with people who are in darkness, our experience will be fear, turmoil, and bondage. The relationships we pursue play a major role in where we end up in life. Pay attention to who you allow in your sphere. Ignoring God and remaining in unequally yoked relationships ultimately results in disaster and leads us to experience His discipline.

When we first begin to study God's Word, most things do not make sense. For example, we must believe before we will ever see. To develop trust and the confidence that God will do what the Word says requires a time commitment from us. We must develop the relationship. The process works, just like any other relationship that we endeavor to develop. During these early stages of our learning, we must first have faith before we are able to see the things we believe in. The walk is one of faith, and it defies all that is taking place in our surroundings.

One of the tools to help develop our relationship with God is using biblical stories to align with our life experiences. The same manner in which God worked back then applies to us today. The study of the Bible works in the same manner as world's education system. In that system, we are using history as a tool to develop our knowledge of how to succeed in the Earth's realm. The difference is that the Bible provides a higher level of wisdom, one that supersedes that of Earth's realm. Getting started might be extremely intimidating. However, with time we not only understand but also we receive insight, coupled with wisdom from above. Once you receive the revelation from God, sin will lose its appeal in your life as long as you continue to feed on the Word daily. After all, the Word of God is the food that the Spirit requires to operate at its fullest potential. At this stage of the development, the desire for anything other than obedience to the Word loses its power over you.

How do we free ourselves from the sinful nature into which we are born?

> You were blameless in all you did from the day you were created
> until evil was found in you.
> —EZEKIEL 28:15

How do we attract surroundings conducive to bringing light into our lives? Use of the Guidebook is the only effective way to accomplish this monumental commission. God never changes; His light chases away the darkness. Earth's population is comprised mostly of followers. Look around. This is very easy to spot. It takes one person in darkness to create conduct that is deemed good, and people flock to emulate such behavior. It's called style, cool, hip, or fun, and the world jumps on the bandwagon. We need to recognize that the world's population is in a state of revolt and needs propping up.

Humanity's ignorance, coupled with rebellion against the biblical teachings, is cause for major concern. We are experiencing the same form of rebellion displayed in the Bible, which showed its ugly face when God brought down the wrath on the nation of Israel. God does not change. There will always be a consequence for sin by both individuals and nations.

> "Lord help!" They cried in their trouble, and he saved them from their
> distress. He led them straight to safety, to a city where they could
> live…They rebelled against the words of God, scorning the counsel
> of the Most High. That is why he broke them with hard labor; they
> fell, and no one helped them rise again.
> —PSALM 107:6–7, 11–12

Our sinful nature does not allow for anything other than self-centered behavior. Unless we acknowledge our Creator, receive Him as Lord to be ushered in under the banner of the kingdom of God, we will remain in darkness. Without acceptance, we are unable to receive cleansing from the sinful nature we were born under through no fault of our own. Darkness is only able to attract dark surroundings, which ultimately lead to destruction.

> I must remind you—and you know it well—that even though
> the Lord rescued the whole nation of Israel from Egypt, he later
> destroyed every one of those who did not remain faithful.
> —JUDE 1:5

By walking in godly wisdom we avoid wrath.

> Whoever walks with the wise will become wise; whoever walks
> with fools will suffer harm.
> —PROVERBS 13:20

WISDOM IS CALLING

There were times in life when I walked with people who the Bible would deem as fools, and I was completely in ignorance to what I was doing. I was surrounding myself with people who were in darkness. At the same time, I was preventing myself from experiencing love, peace, and joy. We live in a very dark world, and unless we arm ourselves with the Word of God, there is no assurance that we will recognize the fools who come into our sphere. We must be mindful and pay attention to those relationships we choose to allow or pursue in our lives.

I attended a church many years ago where I now realize that I was connected with fools, and it stunted my spiritual growth. I was caught up in doing things that quite honestly had nothing to do with God. Why? They were not Holy Spirit directed. I left the church after two years. I now realize that I wasted precious time. Had I been grounded in God's Word, as I am now, I could have avoided that path. Without the wisdom of God, no matter how high our IQ, we will ultimately get caught up in darkness.

> Come here and listen to me! I'll pour out the spirit of wisdom
> upon you and make you wise.
> —PROVERBS 1:23

In speaking of wisdom, I reference the kingdom of God's standard, not that of humanity. Most people equate wisdom with financial opulence or an advanced educational level, but they are missing the mark. Money without knowing God is completely fruitless.

> There is one who makes himself rich, yet has nothing.
> —PROVERBS 13:7, KJV

The standard of wisdom of the kingdom of God was the one He intended for us to emulate in the Earth's realm. When this standard is used, we will always exceed all earthly expectations, as it is the highest measurement for all areas in our life. I thank God for those soldiers in the army of the kingdom who remain committed to pray for the betterment of earth's population and enlightenment of biblical truth. Prayer is the only means of keeping more of the wrath of God from descending upon us.

Humanity defines *wisdom* as "the correct use of knowledge and information," while God's definition of it is "the ability to identify things from His viewpoint and respond to them based on the principles outlined in Scripture." How do we acquire godly wisdom? The call comes when we experience perils in our lives. It was during one of those wisdom calls from the spirit of God within that the great I Am said to me, "I am the only one that is able to provide the path to freedom from bondage. How? My Word is the wisdom I have outlined for believers." The wisdom from God is the master key to open the doors to His treasures. The following scripture sums it up:

> Listen as wisdom calls out! Hear as understanding raises her voice! She stands on the hilltop and at the crossroads. At the entrance to the city, at the city gates, she cries aloud, "I call to you, to all of you! I am raising my voice to all people. How naive you are! Let me give you common sense. O foolish ones, let me give you understanding. Listen to me! For I have excellent things to tell you. Everything I say is right, for I speak the truth and hate every kind of deception. My advice is wholesome and good. There is nothing crooked or twisted in it. My words are plain to anyone with understanding, clear to those who want to learn. Choose my instruction rather than silver, and knowledge over pure gold. For wisdom is far more valuable than rubies. Nothing you desire can be compared with it. I, Wisdom, live together with good judgment. I know where to discover knowledge and discernment. All who fear the Lord will hate evil. That is why I hate pride, arrogance, corruption, and perverted speech. Good advice and success belong to me. Insight and strength are mine. Because of me, kings reign, and rulers make just laws. Rulers lead with my help, and nobles make righteous judgments. I love all who love me. Those who search for me will surely find me. Unending riches, honor, wealth, and justice are mine to distribute. My gifts are better than the purest gold, my wages better than sterling silver! I walk in righteousness, in paths of justice. Those who love me inherit wealth, for I fill their treasuries."
>
> —Proverbs 8:1–20

It is likely that the problem that frustrates and infuriates you the most is the one God will assign to you to solve. What frustrates you right now? I challenge you to use God's Word to find a solution to the problem that most infuriates you. Our Creator has provided all the tools and resources required to accomplish this assignment. Use them!

OBEDIENCE PROTECTS OUR ENVIRONMENT

When we obey God, He guides our steps and surrounds our loved ones with His protective shield.

> Happy are those who fear the LORD. Yes, happy are those who delight in doing what he commands. Their children will be successful everywhere; an entire generation of godly people will be blessed.
> —PSALM 112:1–2

How do we learn obedience to God's Word? Obedience is learned when we experience pain and receive discipline for not adhering to the laws of the kingdom. In the Earth's realm, there are laws that—if we choose to disobey them—we suffer the consequences for, be it fines, community service, probation, or jail time. The same principle applies in the kingdom of God. Since our time on Earth is only temporary, common sense would lead us to master the laws of eternal life.

God's purpose is for us to live a life developed in faith with an aim to get us there by any means necessary. It is not His intent for us to experience adversity in our lives. However, if that is what it takes to get us to the level of faith He requires, He will allow it. Let us learn from Abram in the Bible, a description of faith in action. (Hebrews 11.)

Abram lived in a society of idol worshipers, very similar to the world today. However, when he received a call from the sovereign God of the universe it got his attention. The following scripture gives us a glimpse of one of the ways God approaches humanity for assignments. This is a specific direction God gave to Abram. God told Abram:

> Leave your country, your relatives, and your father's house, and go to the land that I will show you. I will cause you to become the father of a great nation. I will bless you and make you famous, and I will make you a blessing to others. I will bless those who bless you and curse those who curse you. All the families of the earth will be blessed through you." So Abram departed as the LORD had instructed him,

and Lot went with him. Abram was seventy-five years old when he left Haran. He took his wife, Sarai, his nephew Lot, and all his wealth—his livestock and all the people who had joined his household at Haran—and finally arrived in Canaan. Traveling through Canaan, they came to a place near Shechem and set up camp beside the oak at Moreh. At that time, the area was inhabited by Canaanites. Then the LORD appeared to Abram and said, "I am going to give this land to your offspring."

—GENESIS 12:1–7

How did Abram know it was God? His heart was in a receptive mode. Keep in mind, Abram did not have the Bible as a guide as we do today. However, when he received the call, he paid attention.

Have you ever received a call from God? We all have. However, many of us are not listening, expecting, or paying attention, and therefore we miss it. Directions from our Father come to the believer today in the same manner in which they were dispersed to Abram. Too often in our preoccupation with worldly distractions we miss the call. Are you prepared for a call? Are you expecting to receive a call? Are you receptive enough to know that the Lord is talking to you?

DISOBEDIENCE TAINTS OUR ENVIRONMENT

Our Creator gave two commands to Adam and Eve. First, He told them to fill the earth and rule over it. Second, He told them not to eat from a specific tree in the Garden (Gen. 1:28; 2:17). When they chose to disobey, their relationship with God was severed, and they were forced to leave Eden. This one act of disobedience not only affected their lives, but it also impacted the lives of all future generations. Adam's sin made its entrance into the world, and all of humanity suffered. When we ignore a command from God, we not only affect our own lives but others as well.

We must understand that ignoring a call from God could result in the loss of a blessing for the masses. In my case, I heard a call from God, was receptive to what I had received, and followed direction. I knew enough to know that there was no other choice in the matter. When it relates to God, I adhere to the Word, coupled with the revelation received.

Happy are those who fear the LORD. Yes, happy are those who delight in doing what he commands.

—PSALM 112:1

At times, God's plan requires us to do things that may seem unreasonable. However, His plans are always in line with His will. Initially, I did not take this project to be a reasonable request. But with time, divine revelation came. It came with fear, lots of tears, and, most importantly, prayer. From a logical standpoint, common sense would have been for me to spend every waking moment in pursuit of gainful employment rather than spend time writing a book. However, from a kingdom perspective, the requirement was only:

> Study this Book of the Law continually, Meditate on it day and night so you may be sure to obey all that is written in it. Only then will you succeed.
>
> —JOSHUA 1:8

This book is the product of my obedience to God's will. The following are some basic requirements to follow when walking in faith and obedience.

- Prayer (This is key to develop the relationship.)
- Learn to listen to God.
- Learn to obey God.
- Learn to depend on God.
- Learn to wait on His timing.
- Learn to acknowledge when we have missed the mark.

When we do not listen, God makes us repeat things. When we step ahead of God, we delay and sometimes lose the blessing He has for us. However, when we do what has been revealed, He takes care of the rest.

> And we know that God causes everything to work together for the good of those who love God and are called according to his purpose for them.
>
> —ROMANS 8:28

Once we learn God's ways and have a clear understanding of the consequences of disobedience, the taste of sin becomes so unpleasant. Many people do not believe in a world that exists outside of the reality of what can be seen and touched. God is spirit; hence, we must get to know Him, believe, and have faith, even though we cannot see. Eventually He will allow us to see, through the manifestation of His blessings.

We are made in the image of God; therefore, we are also spirits. Many

Christians have yet to experience the spiritual realm because the journey requires a great deal of commitment. I challenge you to become more than a hearer of God's Word. Be a doer of the Word! Open the Bible and commune with our Creator.

GOD REQUIRES YOUR ATTENTION

Our heavenly Father has provided the resource required to develop a relationship with Him. It is very unfortunate that many people spend an entire lifetime in the Earth's realm without ever knowing their Creator. To ignore this relationship and fail to discover the purpose of our earthly existence would be the greatest loss of opportunity to mankind. Events in the Bible serve to help us understand how God worked in the past and how we can expect Him to work in our life if we give Him access. If what we believe is never tested by adversity, it remains head knowledge. We know it; however, without application to our problem it becomes useless. Until we apply the principles given in the Word of God, we will never know that He can be trusted to perform His Word. As a warning to us, be mindful that God is love, but He hates sin and will discipline when necessary.

> I don't want you to forget, dear brothers and sisters, what happened to our ancestors in the wilderness long ago. God guided all of them by sending a cloud that moved along ahead of them, and he brought them all safely through the waters of the sea on dry ground. As followers of Moses, they were all baptized in the cloud and the sea. And all of them ate the same miraculous food, and all of them drank the same miraculous water. For they all drank from the miraculous rock that traveled with them, and that rock was Christ. Yet after all this, God was not pleased with most of them, and he destroyed them in the wilderness.
>
> —1 CORINTHIANS 10:1–5

Are you one of the many who appear to have things all figured out, yet you remain empty on the inside? Jesus Christ is the only One with the power to redeem you and fill that vacant spot in your soul. Examine your life and discover what is holding you back from seeking the most important relationship in this life. Understanding and living the Word of God is the most valuable investment you will ever make in life. When we become God's tool to be used in the life of others and we are able to be the tool to transfer others from the realm of darkness into the kingdom of light, then we step into the realm of extraordinary. When believers in the body of Christ remain complacent, they jeopardize the destiny of others. How? They hear the Word, and they are saved, but they keep it to themselves.

If you have read this and believe in your heart that now is the right time to make a commitment to your Creator, I would like to provide you with a suggested salvation prayer. If you have never accepted Jesus as your Lord and Savior and wish to do so at this time, it is very simple. It is so easy that many believe that it is too good to be true. It is that easy! Try it! All you need to do is believe it in your heart and say:

> *Heavenly Father, I come to You now. You said, "If you confess with your mouth that Jesus is Lord and believe in your heart God raised him from the dead, you will be saved. For it is by believing in your heart that you are made right with God, and it is by confessing with your mouth that you are saved" (Rom. 10:9–10). Father, I ask You now to come into my heart. I believe that God raised Jesus from the dead. I receive salvation now by faith. I thank You, praise, and give You all the glory for this grace. In Jesus' name, Amen.*

You are now saved, a Christian, a child of almighty God, and a member of the body of Christ. What to do next?

1. Start reading the Bible daily. It is the required daily food for the spirit. You might want to start with the Gospel of John.

2. Start a prayer life. Talk to God like you would to anyone else.

3. Tell someone about Jesus.

4. Connect with a gospel-teaching church.

5. Serve the Lord.

6. Fellowship with other believers.

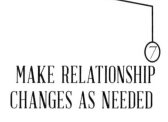

MAKE RELATIONSHIP CHANGES AS NEEDED

RELATIONSHIPS ARE THE most important aspect of our lives. The right relationship can catapult you into success, and the wrong relationship can lead you down a wrong road. Therefore, it is crucial that we surround ourselves with people with integrity and godly wisdom. Why would it be important to make changes in relationships as we grow closer to God? For starters, as we grow in the Word, some of our former relationships may be in conflict with our new position in the light of God. Sometimes family members and friends create barriers to our development process. Since it is not always possible to please God and mankind simultaneously, we must adapt our lives accordingly if we are serious about developing a relationship with God.

When I began my ongoing in-depth conversation with God, it led me to the light of His Word. Many of my friends, family, and people in my sphere of influence were not experiencing the same light and were moving in a different direction in life than me. I found myself having to distance myself from any and everyone who was not a positive influence on my journey. Before long, all those relationships that needed to disappear simply vanished. There was nothing I did or needed to do. God did it for me. When we allow God to guide our thoughts and our lives, He takes responsibility to ensure that we are in right relationships. He brings the right people into our lives and, conversely, takes the wrong people out.

In order to walk in the light, it is important that we walk with people on similar paths. Thus, it behooves us to ensure that we are equally yoked with those in the light. How do we do this? The time to evaluate character in others is before you get too deeply involved. Scripture warns us to be guarded: "Above all else, guard your heart, for it affects everything you do" (Prov. 4:23). We should never compromise our walk in the light. How do we avoid this? We team ourselves with likeminded individuals who share the same spiritual beliefs and values, and we steer clear of those who could potentially take us off our path.

Don't team up with those who are unbelievers. How can goodness
be a partner with wickedness? How can light live with darkness?
What harmony can there be between Christ and the Devil? How
can a believer be a partner with an unbeliever? And what union can
there be between God's temple and idols? For we are the temple of
the living God. As God said: "I will live in them and walk among
them. I will be their God, and they will be my people. Therefore,
come out from them and separate yourselves from them, says the
Lord. Don't touch their filthy things, and I will welcome you. And
I will be your Father, and you will be my sons and daughters, says
the Lord Almighty."

—2 CORINTHIANS 6:14–18

Every relationship we have in life is made possible through Jesus. We
must guard our relationships to avoid wandering into the wilderness. What
do you mean? A relationship usually leads us to God or diverts us in the
opposite direction. Be always mindful of where you're headed and choose
the direction that leads to God. When we are in obedience and faith, all
we have to do follow what God has called us to do, and His grace does for
us supernaturally what we are unable to do for ourselves. The key to this
supernatural intervention is obedience.

Perhaps no story can make the point more clearly about changing our
relationships than the life of Samson. Samson was chosen, separated, and
consecrated to a mission to which God had called him. He was to be the
one God would use to free the Israelites out of the hand of forty years of
Philistine captivity. The life of Samson has always made good Hollywood
copy and stories for Sunday school classes. However, it never delivered a
substantive message to me. Nonetheless, when we take a closer look at the
life of Samson, we see a powerful lesson of hope recorded in the Bible.

In the Old Testament we see a disobedient and idolatrous people suffer
defeat time and again because of people's rebellion against God. The Israelites
did what was evil in the Lord's sight, so the Lord handed them over to the
Philistines, who kept them in subjection for forty years (Judg. 13). During
that time of oppression, Samson was birthed from a mother who was barren.
She and her husband prayed to the Lord for a child, and He answered their
petition. One day she was approached by an angel of the Lord regarding her
plight, and the angel said to her, "Even though you have not been able to have
children, you will soon become pregnant and give birth to a son" (Judg. 13:3).
Pay attention to ordinary encounters. They may actually be with a heavenly
ambassador sent by God. The angel continued providing her with specific

instructions from God: "You must not drink any beer or wine or any other alcoholic drink or eat any forbidden food. You will become pregnant and give birth to a son, and his hair must never be cut. For he will be dedicated to God as a Nazirite from birth" (vv. 4–5). A Nazirite is a person who is consecrated and separated for the service of God. The woman had the baby boy, as the angel of the Lord declared, and called him Samson. Samson was blessed by God and led by His Spirit. Samson's calling from birth was to commence the deliverance of Israel from the Philistine oppression.

Why was this couple chosen for this assignment? Perhaps brokenness was the qualifier. They were in great emotional pain because of a lack of ability to obtain the desires of their heart, a child. Brokenness is a time when we are able to be of maximum use to the kingdom of God. It occurs after we do all that we know to do in our own human strength. Then, in desperation, we turn to God. From my study of the Word of God, when we surrender and remain in obedience He takes responsibility for the outcome.

In the midst of a disobedient nation, this couple stood out. Why? They sought God's counsel of how to rear their son in most difficult times. Even with their excellent rearing, the child still had human weaknesses.

Samson had a weakness for women, which proved to be his downfall. After he grew up, Samson traveled to a nearby town and saw a beautiful woman named Delilah. When he returned home, he told his father, "I have seen a Philistine woman in Timnah; now get her for me as my wife" (Jud. 14:2, NIV). His father protested, "Isn't there one woman in our tribe or among all the Israelites you could marry? Why must you go to the pagan Philistines to find a wife?" (v. 3). Why would his father suggest this? Unequally yoked union leads to darkness. Nevertheless, he gave in and arranged for Samson to meet her. Eventually Samson disregarded his parents and married Delilah. Samson's desire for a Philistine wife was clearly transgression against God's law. However, God used Samson's disobedience for the good of His people.

When Samson fell in love with Delilah, it marked the beginning of His downfall and eventual demise. (See Judges 16.) It did not take long for the rich and powerful Philistine rulers to bribe her to find out the secret of his strength. The adversary is continuously working to derail God's plans. Using the powers of seduction and deception, Delilah wore Samson down with her persistent requests. Finally, she wore him down, and he foolishly told her about the power of his strength regarding the vow he took never to cut his hair. While Samson was asleep, Delilah called her coconspirators to shave his hair. In his weakness, Samson was captured. Rather than kill him, the Philistines preferred to humiliate him. Samson was blinded and subjected to hard labor in a Gaza prison.

As he slaved in the prison, his hair grew back. However, the careless Philistines paid no attention. In spite of his failure and sin of major consequence, Samson was now humbled. He prayed to God, and God answered his prayers. In repentance, an idea took shape in Samson's mind, one last mighty act for God. Divine power surged through the strong man's limbs, and he brought a greater disaster on Israel's enemies than ever before.

Samson's hair was not the source of his power. It was merely an outward sign that his life was set apart for God's service. When Samson divulged the secret of his strength to Delilah, he betrayed his relationship with God. Have you ever betrayed your relationship with God? Why? Was it for instant gratification? For Samson, what started as a grand life with God was derailed because of his choice of relationships and his loss of focus.

The life of Samson is a prime example of what happens when we allow worldly pursuits to derail us from our preordained destinies. We are human, so flesh often gets in the way of where our focus needs to be. Pay attention. Like Samson, we know that when we give ourselves over to sin, we open ourselves up to be deceived. It is not possible to see truth where there is sin. God never honors sin. Spiritually, Samson lost his calling from God and gave up his greatest gift, his physical strength, to please the woman who captured his affections. In the end, it cost him physical sight, his freedom, his dignity, and eventually his life. Samson compromised his relationship with God and missed his call.

I challenge you to evaluate your relationships. We were all created in the image of God with the same potential to carry out the supernatural with grace. However, be mindful that every good thing comes from God. The kingdom of God is one of seeds. However, we are each given the ability to sow seeds of obedience or disobedience. We are able to choose life or death. Like Samson, when we place other things ahead of God's mandate, discipline will fall upon us.

Reading the account of Samson's life and his downfall with Delilah, one might consider his life a failure. Yet, he accomplished the mission that God assigned him. What is the moral to the story? Guard yourself from destructive relationships and make changes as required to remain in the light. Are you in obedience to God? We become like the people we associate with.

> Whoever walks with the wise becomes wise; whoever walks with fools will suffer harm.
> —PROVERBS 13:20

God would have been able to accomplish so much more through Samson's wholehearted obedience. At the end, Samson requested restoration of his strength, not for self-serving reasons but to carry out God's will. In today's time, what can you take from this?

PART 3:
SURRENDER IN GOD'S PRESENCE
Rest in the Finished Work

IN SURRENDER GOD IS
OUR COMPANION

WHEN WE COME into the world, we come forth with no attachments. We come with the expectations that our needs will be met. However, as we commence the journey, we become encircled with boundaries. We then become attached to a belief system that creates and controls our entire thought process unless we discover our true purpose in life and change course. Our treasure in God has been deposited in the Guidebook. Surrender makes it possible to tap into the Spirit within, which is the key to the storehouse. Surrender requires us to do much more than sit idle, waiting for God to do something. It requires us to have clarity of who we are in Christ. Unless this is uncovered, we will be forever connected to the world's nominal standards of operation.

At some point we all develop egos, and unfortunately they play a major role in our sense of self, at times to our detriment. Many of us find it very difficult to release our egos, and even when we do, we never permanently get rid of it. For me, once I implemented the Bible in my daily life as my premier source for direction, I managed to suppress my ego and yield to God's will. In order to completely surrender our egos, we must work at it daily.

God has never commanded us to do anything that He has not already equipped us to do. He has given us His Word and will honor all that is stated in it. Faith, obedience, and trust are the major prerequisites.

> And I will give you a new heart with new and right desires, and I will put a new spirit in you. I will take out your stony heart of sin and give you a new, obedient heart.
> —EZEKIEL 36:26

> Forever, O LORD, your word stands firm in heaven.
> —PSALM 119:89

What is surrender? To surrender is "to yield something to the possession or power of another."[1] It is to take our hand off the wheel and allow God to drive. *Surrender* is the perfect Word to describe how we are to respond to the gospel. However, before we are able to submit our total being—mind, body, and soul—we need to understand what it all means. If Jesus is Lord, then surrender to His control of our lives is exactly what is expected of us, but to surrender without knowing the laws of the kingdom is fruitless. How do we surrender? In surrender we allow the part of God within us to control and guide us. It is the point where our force or resistance ceases to function; we cannot help but respond to the call of God's spirit. We release our own selfish desires and allow God's will to reign over us. What God is looking for us to do is to surrender our sin, and in exchange He will give us righteousness.

> I myself no longer live, but Christ lives in me. So I live my life in this earthly body by trusting in the Son of God, who loved me and gave himself for me.
>   —GALATIANS 2:20

During this experience of releasing our need to control, we allow love to make all decisions and the peace of God to tell us where to go, who to see, and what to say. It is a point of rest in knowing when we have done all that we can do and then trusting God to finish the work. We then allow the part of us that is God to shine.

Many of us in the Christian community are clearly saved. However, we have not taken the next step to operate in full surrender with the Lord. As a result we have one foot in the kingdom and the other in the earthly world.

> So humble yourselves therefore to God. Resist the Devil, and he will flee from you.
>   —JAMES 4:7

The major problem with this is that we cannot serve God and man simultaneously. Therefore, a large portion of our time is spent in busying ourselves with self-serving activities that have absolutely nothing to do with God. The outcome is that we never find our true divine destiny in life. We miss most of the important blessings that being led by the Spirit provides, such as discovering our true calling or even receiving a revelation of who our true life partner should be. The only way to be in the center of God's perfect will, while in the Earth's realm, is to know kingdom laws and surrender to them.

Surrender is being in the world but not of it. What does that mean? It is living in this world while being fully in tune to follow direction and guidance from your spirit.

> Stop loving this evil world and all that it offers you, for when you love the world, you show that you do not have the love of the Father in you.
>
> —1 John 2:15

This is the place where, in the midst of all the evil around, the evil does not necessarily affect us. We have been supernaturally transplanted into the kingdom of God. Disconnect from the world's standards and develop and follow those of the kingdom. Since Jesus purchased our freedom by becoming a curse for us, this should be the determining factor for us to change our ways from takers to givers. We all have a responsibility to get on board.

Redemption through Jesus' dying on the cross connects us back to the Spirit of God, which we lost when Adam sinned. The spiritual realm was created by God and has dominion over all Earth. Adam's sin separated Earth's population from the spiritual world, but Jesus reopened connection by shedding His own blood. Because the spiritual realm has dominion over all the Earth, we can take comfort in knowing that God will honor His Word and give us rest when we surrender to His will. Jesus said, "Come to me, all of you who are weary and carry heavy burdens, and I will give you rest. Take my yoke upon you. Let me teach you, because I am humble and gentle, and you will find rest for your souls. For my yoke fits perfectly, and the burden I give you is light" (Matt. 11:28–30). Is there anyone on Earth that can provide such assurance?

God is the fountain of life, the only true Source of power and goodness in the Earth's realm. Throughout the universe all that is good comes from God. God has created the sun, moon, stars, flowers, and trees. Are these not all surrendered to God?

> So I tell you, don't worry about everyday life—whether you have enough food, drink, and clothes. Doesn't life consist of more than food and clothing? Look at the birds. They don't need to plant or harvest or put food in barns because your heavenly Father feeds them. And you are far more valuable to him than they are. Can all your worries add a single moment to your life? Of course not. And why worry about your clothes? Look at the lilies and how they grow. They don't work or make their clothing, yet Solomon in all his glory was not dressed as beautifully as they are. And if God cares so wonderfully for flowers that are here today and gone tomorrow, won't he more surely care for you? You have so little faith! So don't worry about having enough food or drink or

clothing. Why be like the pagans who are so deeply concerned about these things? Your heavenly Father already knows all your needs, and he will give you all you need from day to day if you live for him and make the Kingdom of God your primary concern. So don't worry about tomorrow, for tomorrow will bring its own worries. Today's trouble is enough for today.

—MATTHEW 6:25–34

God will supply every single need when we surrender. We do not have what we need because we are not claiming our promises in His Word. I challenge you to become acquainted with the Guidebook for eternal life.

The truth of God's Word provides:

+ Guidance,

+ Wisdom,

+ Courage,

+ Comfort, and

+ Faith.

God is looking for a body of believers who will take Him at His Word. The Old Testament was a foreshadowing of things to come. Look at what was accomplished in surrender with men like Abraham. He was the founding father of the Jewish nation of Israel, a man of great faith and obedience to the will of God. Do you think that it was coincidence that God found him? Absolutely not! Abraham was birthed from a generation of idol worshipers. However, his heart was receptive to God's call when he heard the voice. God measures our readiness by way of the heart. God raised Abram, changed his name to Abraham, and prepared him as an instrument for His glory. God wants to do the same with you and me, not necessarily with a change of name but one of heart.

God is looking for people that will take Him up on the offer to surrender to His will. Many are in search of more for their lives, but they know not what. Our heart's longing will never be satisfied without Jesus. He lived a life of complete surrender to the Father while in the Earth's realm. He is living in our heart by His Holy Spirit. He desires to help us understand this truth. Trust God to work His grace of surrender in you. When God has begun the work of absolute surrender, and when He accepts your surrender, then He holds Himself responsible for the outcome of your triumphs and your perils. Jesus prayed this for us believers: "My prayer for all of them is that they will be one, just as you and I are one, Father—that just as you are in me and I am in you, so they will be in us, and the world will believe you sent me" (John 17:21).

Surrender and Rest in God's Presence

We are only able to rest in God's presence in surrender. In surrender we are imbued with power, which comes from the Spirit. Think of yourself surrendering to God, the same as a tree being attached to its branches. The tree has no other choice than to be surrendered in order to maintain its fruitfulness. If the branches are severed from the tree it ceases to be fruitful. One of the main reasons why the body of Christ is not producing much fruit is because it has lost union with the Spirit of God. Only in surrender can we bear fruit.

> I am the true vine, and my Father is the gardener. He cuts off every branch that doesn't produce fruit, and he prunes the branches that do bear fruit so they will produce even more. You have already been pruned for greater fruitfulness by the message I have given you. Remain in me, and I will remain in you. For a branch cannot produce fruit if it is severed from the vine, and you cannot be fruitful apart from me. Yes, I am the vine; you are the branches. Those who remain in me, and I in them, will produce much fruit. For apart from me you can do nothing.
>
> —John 15:1–5

At some point, we will all surrender to God. Some of us will choose to do it voluntarily while in the Earth's realm. Others will do so forcefully when the body ceases to exist in the flesh. For now, like salvation, surrender is a gift we are free to either accept or reject. Many Christians would not begin to consider surrender and rest in God. Why? God is a stranger to most. During a fellowship experience at church one day, someone said to me, "I have a problem with God thinking He knows what is best for me better than I do. Therefore, surrender is not possible for me." I was extremely saddened by the comment. It became very clear that although this individual was very active in church attendance and activities, she had no relationship with the Father. When believers are in relationship with the Father and are doers of the Word, His omniscience would never be in question. In surrender, the Spirit of God supplies all the necessary discernment to carry out the will of God, and all that is required is furnished to us. Although darkness sprouts up on occasion, it will never overtake us, because we have been delivered out of the world's darkness into the kingdom of light.

Our flesh is the part of us clamoring for independence from God. God will take care when we surrender. Surrender causes blessings to come forth. It is possible that you might not have as clear a point of view of surrender as you would like to because of where you are in the journey. However, this is the perfect time to humble yourself in God's sight and acknowledge that you have grieved the Holy Spirit by demanding your own way.

> Commit your work to the LORD, and then your plans will succeed. The LORD has made everything for his own purposes, even the wicked for punishment.
> —PROVERBS 16:3–4

CONSEQUENCES OF NOT SURRENDERING

The place of surrender is the space where we are open to receive guidance from God's Spirit within the believer. The Holy Spirit is our Helper and guides us with interpretation of the truth of God. God speaks to us in complete alignment with Scripture. We cannot follow direction if we do not know the Word. Events in the Bible are recorded so that we might learn from past mistakes. When we ignore a call from God the result could turn to be lethal. How so? Let us take a look at Jonah's experience and learn from it.

Jonah received a call from God to preach repentance to the people of Nineveh (Jonah 1–2). Instead of obeying, he went to Joppa to board a ship to the city of Tarshish. Jonah's disobedience brought punishment upon himself and others around him. After he boarded the ship to Tarshish there was a great storm. During the storm, the men working on the ship began calling upon their gods and idols to deliver them from whatever punishment was being given. The workers found Jonah in the bottom of the ship asleep. They awakened him and asked him to pray to his God for protection.

These men cast lots to see who brought the punishment upon them. The lot fell upon Jonah. He confessed that he was a Hebrew and was running away from God. Jonah asked the men to throw him overboard. Instead they tried hard to bring the ship to land. Jonah finally convinced them that he was the one who brought judgment from God. The sailors agreed to throw him into the sea. As soon as they did, the storm broke, and the water was calm. Jonah landed in the water and was swallowed by a great fish. He was in the whale's belly for three days and three nights. Jonah prayed to the Lord from inside of the fish. Then the Lord ordered the fish to spit up Jonah on the beach, and it did.

God's intent for Jonah was not death. Instead, it was a lesson in discipline due to his disobedience. The Holy Spirit deals with believers on the basis of their relationship with Jesus and convicts us for disobedience to the Lord. Like Jonah, I have also received discipline from the Lord because of decisions not aligned to His will. It is important to know that God's Spirit penetrates our heart and brings awareness of wrongdoing. The action to take is repent and immediately fall back in line with His will.

Are you ignoring a command from God? It is absolutely impossible to ignore God and get away with it.

> Don't copy the behavior and customs of this world, but let God transform you into a new person by changing the way you think. Then you will know what God wants you to do, and you will know how good and pleasing and perfect his will really is.
>
> —Romans 12:2

Victory in Surrender

When I initially determined to surrender fully to God, I had no idea what to expect. I knew from my study of the Word that faith, coupled with obedience, were major requirements for fully understanding and being one with the kingdom of God. What I was most afraid of was not the obedience aspect but what I might be asked to do. My first thought was, What if I am unable to deliver? It then dawned on me that any request coming from God would be accomplished in His strength, not my own. Once it became clear that I was only the vessel, my fears lessened.

When I received the assignment to write this book, it was way beyond anything I thought I was capable of doing. How did the assignment come to me? One day God sent a messenger to my home. The messenger was someone I had not seen in several years. My phone rang, and the person said, "I am in your city, and I would like to drop by your home in fifteen minutes." I said OK. When the person arrived, she said, "I only have a few minutes. I have a message for you. God wants you to write a book." I asked, "Regarding?" "He wants you to share how you endured seven years of unemployment with complete focus on the Word of God. Additionally, He also wants you talk about the learning you have developed regarding biblical solutions for our everyday concerns and share it with others," she said. I was stunned. Shortly thereafter, she left.

Initially, I was confounded. Had I not been a ten-year student of God's Word, I might have dismissed the message. But in this instance I knew I could not. The major reason I paid attention was because the messenger was a person living in the light of God. I knew that through prayer and meditation I would receive some direction concerning the message. From my study of the Word of God I learned that He deals with us in the areas in which we are the most fearful. In my case, one of my greatest fears was writing. I prayed and said, "God I need to hear from you."

The following night, the revelation to write the book came through divine discernment, a spiritual awareness—when you know that you know that you know that the Creator has spoken to you personally. Initially, He provided the name of the book in a dream. I went as far as to say to God, "I need a sign that this is really You." In my mind I said, "I will go into Staples in search of a flash drive. If one is readily accessible and on sale for less than ten dollars, then that will be my confirmation that it is from God."

I arrived at Staples the next morning, and there was a sales person at the door. I asked, "Sir, do you have a flash drive on sale?" Low and behold, it was on a rack at the checkout station on sale for a little under ten dollars. I purchased the flash drive, got in my car and said, "Yes! Yes, this is God." I was overjoyed and thought to myself, "God is talking to me."

Over the course of the next few nights, in a series of dreams, He revealed eleven topic titles He wanted me to cover in the book. I got out of bed and recorded the eleven titles. Regarding the meat of the chapters, He provided discernment with messages from visions, Scripture, sermons, and Holy Spirit promptings. Although I did not believe I was qualified for the job, I knew that God was and that He would give me the tools I needed. I believe at this point God knew He could trust me to be obedient to the call.

Studying God's Word is the first step to learning His ways. When you know the Word it makes it easier to hear the call. Only God knows what the outcome of this assignment will be. My job is to listen, trust, and obey.

I believe that one of the most difficult things in the life of a Christian is to surrender complete control to the promptings of the Holy Spirit. Without surrender it is impossible to be in complete harmony with the spirit of God. Surrender only becomes possible when we have pursued God and gotten to know Him from revelations received in Scripture.

> But seek first his kingdom and his righteousness, and all these
> things will be given to you as well.
> —MATTHEW 6:33, NIV

Surrender only became possible to me when God's Word came alive in my spirit. The Word of God is food for the spirit. Hence, we need to feed on the Word daily. As I continue to meditate on Scripture, it keeps me focused on the priorities of life.

There are multiple reasons why we should all surrender to God!

1. God is omniscient.
2. God is omnipotent.
3. God is omnipresent.
4. God is truthful.
5. God is immutable.

We were created to be in relationship with God and experience His power at work in our lives. However, it requires work on our part, particularly reading the Word. It requires more than saying, "I am a Christian." It is more than going to church once a week. We are not useful to the kingdom of God if we do not know the Word of God.

Why would anyone give up an opportunity to be in relationship with our Redeemer, Protector, and Provider, the One who knows the beginning and the end? There are some incredible blessings that God will bestow upon those who are willing to follow Him in full surrender. These benefits are not only in this life but also in the eternal life.

Do you know that God is thinking about you? He has plans for you.

> "For I know the plans I have for you," says the Lord. "They are plans for good and not for disaster, to give you a future and a hope."
> —Jeremiah 29:11

In view of God's plan for you, can you think of one reason *not* to surrender? No one—including those who worship other gods and idols—is able to make changes to the plans the God of Israel has predestined for us.

> From eternity to eternity I am God; No one can oppose what I do. No one can reverse my actions.
> —Isaiah 43:13

In surrender, all of our life's burdens, perils, and adversities are released to our Creator's hands, where they belong. The burden is not ours; it is the Lord's.

> Give your burdens to the Lord, and he will take care of you. He will not permit the godly to slip and fall.
> —Psalm 55:22

⑨ WHO IS LEADING YOU?

Listening to God is essential to being led by God. We need to learn that we are here to listen to God.

> Be quick to listen, slow to speak, and slow to get angry. Your anger can never make things right in God's sight. So get rid of all the filth and evil in your lives, and humbly accept the message God has planted in your hearts, for it is strong enough to save your souls.
>
> —James 1:19–21

We cannot lose when we are led by the Spirit of God. In order to know where we are going, we need to pay attention to who we are listening to and who we are following.

> And be sure to pay attention to what you hear. The more you do this, the more you will understand—and even more, besides.
>
> —Mark 4:24

Discovery from the Spirit of God comes down to us by way of our heart. Only those born-again believers have access to receiving this guidance. Why? Based on our Creator's commitment to adhere to integrity to the covenant, He will never renege on the promises He made. We have been given the choice to rebel or believe. When we believe, we opt for the light of God. When we rebel, we elect darkness and the wicked ways of the world. The message coming from our heart will be of light and peace if they are coming from Him. If the message is turmoil and darkness it is assuredly of the flesh. Listen to your heart! The process of listening to your heart for God is called discernment. This practice is accomplished with reflection, prayer, conversation, and openness. It is a time-consuming course of action. However, it will confidently answer the question of who is leading you.

Who controls your decisions? Whomever or whatever controls your thoughts is the person or the thing that will lead you. Our Creator has given us free will. However, at times God will intercede to accommodate His will for humanity. Do not be deceived; our spiritual capacity is neither based on education nor intellect. It is measured only by faith and the promises of God in His Word. In order to understand who is leading us, we need to know who we are in Christ. We live in a body, and we possess a soul. One of the requirements for life in the Earth's realm is to possess a body. We are all spirit beings, whether or not we believe in God. However, only those who believe the Messiah have activated the spirit man. When we accept Christ, our spirit is renewed. Supernaturally, we become a new person, alive with God.

> What this means is that those who become Christians become new persons. They are not the same anymore, for the old life is gone. A new life has begun!
>
> —2 Corinthians 5:17

> It is God who saved us and chose us to live a holy life. He did this not because we deserved it, but because that was his plan long before the world began—to show his love and kindness to us through Christ Jesus. And now he has made all of this plain to us by the coming of Christ Jesus, our Savior, who broke the power of death and showed us the way to everlasting life through the Good News.
>
> —2 Timothy 1:9–10

In order to appreciate this section, it is important that we understand what it means to walk in the flesh and to walk in the Spirit. Humanity has been given the freedom to either walk by the Spirit (the light of God) or the flesh (the body following the world's evil ways in darkness). Allow me to share some insight on both.

> I advise you to live according to your new life in the Holy Spirit. Then you won't be doing what your sinful nature craves.
>
> —Galatians 5:17

Operating in the flesh is what we do in our own power, in our own strength. It is what we do for ourselves. Our body—the flesh part of us—is able to accomplish much on its own. However, the accomplishment means very little to God, because the work is usually self-serving and not aligned with the will of God for humanity. We are serving an eternal God. For this reason, our objectives need to align with those of His kingdom.

> The eternal God is your refuge, and his everlasting arms are under
> you. He thrusts out the enemy before you; it is he who cries,
> "Destroy them!"
> —DEUTERONOMY 33:27

At some point in our lives we will find ourselves in the midst of a difficult situation. However, we should never allow the situation to get inside us. Do not allow the flesh part of you to dictate the outcome. Instead, seek guidance from the Spirit of God.

WALKING IN THE SPIRIT

How do we walk by the Spirit? Only through salvation are we able to partake of this joyous experience. The walk is a minute-by-minute walking in complete dependence on our Creator. We walk by faith. We read the Word, meditate, and allow Scripture to renew our minds. This is the place where the majority of the Christian community is stuck. There is a lack of awareness of where to place dependence. Therefore, we continue looking to the world system to meet our needs. The more we focus our dependence on God, the more consistent we become in trusting in Him and walking in the Spirit.

> We can gather our thoughts; but the LORD gives the right answer.
> —PROVERBS 16:1

Without study of the Word of God we follow ideology and ignore Scripture. By reading Scripture we learn that we have been called to freedom. We cannot prosper in God without the anointing of Jesus. We cannot continue to allow the world standards to dictate the way we live our lives. The world is missing the key element to a life of peace, the Word of God—the sword of the Spirit suggestion!

> For no one can lay any other foundation than the one we already
> have—Jesus Christ.
> —1 CORINTHIANS 3:11

Had I not been a student of God's Word, the message for this assignment would have been a foreign language to me. I would have missed the message.

Christianity will not be understood apart from the tripartite nature of man. God is Spirit, and since we were created in His image, we are also spirits. We have a spirit, a soul, and we live in a body. In man's desire to satisfy the needs of the flesh he loses sight of immortality. Once we accept Jesus as Lord we have committed to the call of immortality.

> For God is Spirit, so those who worship him must worship in spirit and in truth.
>
> —John 4:24

Think for a moment, if you were to move to a country whose inhabitants spoke a different language, would you not need to learn their language in order to communicate? The same applies in the spirit realm. In order to communicate and receive from God, we need to speak the kingdom's language. We must speak the language of the spirit, which is God's Word.

> It is the Spirit who gives eternal life. Human effort accomplishes nothing. And the very words I have spoken to you are spirit and life.
>
> —John 6:63

Many only speak to God when things are not going well. The more time we spend in ignorance, ignoring the voice of the Lord, the longer it takes to become activated into the kingdom culture. The spirit of man lies dormant until we ask Jesus to come into our life, at which point our spirit becomes active. When this spirit is activated, the feeling of emptiness many experience disappears. I believe the greatest challenge of every Christian is the struggle of the walk in spirit.

We must exercise those spiritual disciplines that are required to maintain focus on God and away from sin. Study the Word and meditate so that we might not entertain the lust of the flesh. Our Creator's awesomeness is discovered when we develop dependence on Him. The experience exceeds that of any other relationship in the Earth's realm.

> So I say, live by the Spirit, and you will not gratify the desires of the sinful nature. For the sinful nature desires what is contrary to the Spirit, and the Spirit what is contrary to the sinful nature. They are in conflict with each other, so that you do not do what you want.
>
> —Galatians 5:16–17, niv

We become aware of His presence, and He becomes the center of our time. Once our concentration is totally in Him, we remove ourselves from the responsibility of taking control, and we make God responsible for the outcome. Once we make God responsible, we must rid ourselves of distractions that might hinder the outcome. This allows us to exercise the spiritual discipline required to keep our heart focused on Him.

In order to accomplish this monumental walk successfully we need to open up the Bible, study God's Word, and practice obedience. Once we become aware of His ways, the rest of the journey becomes more peaceful. At this juncture in the relationship, somehow, supernaturally, faith increases, and all our worldly desires dissipate. God accomplishes this in the most subtle way. It occurs like salvation, by the grace of God. The favor that God provides us is undeserved and unearned. We can neither work for it nor pay for it.

> God saved you by his special favor when you believed. And you can't take credit for this; it is a gift from God. Salvation is not a reward for the good things we have done, so none of us can boast about it. For we are God's masterpiece. He has created us anew in Christ Jesus, so that we can do the good things he planned for us long ago.
> —EPHESIANS 2:8–10

WALKING IN THE FLESH

It is a great tragedy that many people go through life without ever becoming acquainted with their Creator. To miss this extraordinary relationship is to overlook the purpose of our earthy existence and forsake the most powerful bond in the Earth's realm. When we miss this relationship, our earthly life is spent walking in the flesh. How do we walk in the flesh? The flesh is the spirit within us that desires to act independently from God, so operating according to the flesh is all that we are able to do in our own human power. The flesh is completely apart from God, and when we are led by it, we give in to self-serving agendas. An awareness that we are living from the flesh only comes with a revelation of light from God. This is most difficult if not impossible to explain.

This may sound a bit cliché. However, since the Lord only reveals Himself in the Word, that is the most logical place to start. My revelation came during a life-altering experience. During that time, as an alternative to looking at mere man for help, I chose God as the solution to my problem. In choosing God's Word, I made Him responsible for the outcome. This happened within a period of six months of spending five to six hours a day engulfed in the Word. This may seem like a lot of time to most, but revelation surfaced for me in this manner. Consider that many spend this much time daily between televisions and other social media activities. Why not invest the time in something that offers eternal value?

Think for a minute. We are made in the image of God, which means that we are given the same privileges as Jesus. When children are born into a family they pretty much emulate parental behavior unless they are taught differently. Think of a family where all are farmers, doctors, lawyers, preachers, government workers, or in the entertainment industry. What do the offspring do? In many instances they follow in their parents' footsteps, unless they are otherwise directed or a passion for something develops. Likewise, due to the fact that the Creator of the universe made us in His image, we have the potential to be just like Jesus. How? Through spiritual discovery. This, in most cases, is only revealed during periods of adversity.

When we make decisions from the flesh, then God cannot be held responsible for the outcome. When we walk in the flesh, we sever our ties with the holy One. To walk in the flesh is to go through life depending on mere human abilities and strength. Although many have been fortunate to accumulate much in their own strength, in the end, it all results to be meaningless. The flesh is able to do many things, leading us to create admiration from others. However, many end up in rebellion to God because their motives are usually self-serving.

To live by the flesh is to depend upon the resources and abilities of mere man. To live in the Spirit is to depend upon the resources and abilities that God gives by grace through faith. No one is able to avoid the struggle between the flesh and the Spirit. Further, none of us is able to live a Christian life free of perils. We walk the road daily with awareness to ensure we stay on the right track. Unless we purposely walk in spiritual awareness, the flesh will lead our actions. We were created with a tendency toward the flesh, so unless we are walking in consciousness and renew our mind to line up with the Spirit, our responses will emerge from darkness.

> When you follow the desires of your sinful nature, your lives will produce these evil results: sexual immorality, impure thoughts, eagerness for lustful pleasure, idolatry, participation in demonic activities, hostility, quarreling, jealousy, outbursts of anger, selfish ambition, divisions, the feeling that everyone is wrong except those in your own little group, envy, drunkenness, wild parties, and other kinds of sin. Let me tell you again, as I have before, that anyone living that sort of life will not inherit the Kingdom of God. But when the Holy Spirit controls our lives, he will produce this kind of fruit in us: love, joy, peace, patience, kindness, goodness, faithfulness, gentleness, and self-control. Here there is no conflict with the law.
>
> —Galatians 5:19–23

Who is leading your life?

DISCOVER YOUR AUTHORITY

Without knowing the authority given to us in Christ, we are automatically being led by the flesh, because we have no inkling of the promises of God and the requirements to receive them.

> Now listen! Today I am giving you a choice between prosperity and disaster, between life and death.
> —DEUTERONOMY 30:15

You choose!

Authority can only be implemented when it's known. Consider this: If there were ten million dollars deposited in a bank account for you, yet you did not know it was there, you would not know to make a withdrawal. The same applies to God's kingdom. There are promises from which many believers have not benefited because they do not know about them. Many Christians are in churches every week, but they never read the Bible. They seem to operate with the mentality that it is their pastor's responsibility to read the Bible and share it with the congregation. However, that is not enough to build and maintain a personal, intimate relationship with God. I challenge you to take some time and discover all that the Creator of the universe prepared for you before the beginning of time. Step up to a higher level in your earthly existence.

> Jesus came and told his disciples, "I have been given complete authority in heaven and on earth."
> —MATTHEW 28:18

Jesus is the visible image of the invisible God. Through His work on the cross, we have been given the authority to bring things that were not into existence. Many in the Earth's realm think of authority in terms of professional status and monetary wealth. I assure you that has absolutely nothing to do with the true power given by God. No position or amount of money can offer more protection than the power that comes forth from God's Word. When a believer speaks the Word of God, he is speaking with the authority God has given us.

> You put us in charge of everything you made, giving us authority over all things.
> —PSALM 8:6

Then God said, "Let us make people in our image, to be like ourselves. They will be masters over all life—the fish in the sea, the birds in the sky, and all the livestock, wild animals, and small animals."

—GENESIS 1:26

I am the Alpha and the Omega, the First and the Last, the Beginning and the End.

—REVELATION 22:13

Authority was given to all believers so that we might use it in service to accomplish our Creator's will in the Earth's realm. I only became aware of my authority when I pursued God, read His Word, and received the revelation.

HOW DO WE SERVE?

The way to show our love for God is to serve one another genuinely. For those of us who have an intimate relationship with our Creator, think of all the wisdom we have from God that we could pass on to those around us. There is always someone in need, and we do not need to look very far to lend a helping hand. The splendor of sharing love is that there is no need to ponder; just act. Jesus served others in such extraordinary ways as a means of showing us how to do the same.

When God's children are in need, be the one to help them out. And get into the habit of inviting guests home for dinner or, if they need lodging, for the night.

—ROMANS 12:13

Do we really serve others with kindness? Are our motives aligned with goodness? When we walk in the flesh, we cannot serve any other way but in darkness. The flesh walk is a very effortless journey. Why? The main requirement is to become a follower of the mass populous. Sadly enough, during this phase, people change their values to obtain acceptance. In contrast, service, which is motivated by the Spirit, is delivered selflessly and humbly. The only standard we are accountable to adhere to is that of the kingdom of God. In this case, there is never a need for compromise because kingdom values exceed those of the Earth's realm. Once we serve according to kingdom of God principles we are able to deliver the extraordinary. For me, it took harsh conditions for this message to sink in. Currently and moving forward, God's Word has my undivided attention. I challenge you to make time for God daily.

A SPIRIT-LED LIFE LEADS TO BLESSINGS

When we choose love, we supernaturally transplant ourselves into the mode of receiving blessings from God.

> If I could speak in any language in heaven or on earth but didn't love others, I would only be making meaningless noise like a loud gong or a clanging cymbal. If I had the gift of prophecy, and if I knew all the mysteries of the future and knew everything about everything, but didn't love others, what good would I be? And if I had the gift of faith so that I could speak to a mountain and make it move, without love I would be no good to anybody. If I gave everything I have to the poor and even sacrificed my body, I could boast about it; but if I didn't love others, I would be of no value whatsoever. Love is patient and kind. Love is not jealous or boastful or proud or rude. Love does not demand its own way. Love is not irritable, and it keeps no record of when it has been wronged. It is never glad about injustice but rejoices whenever the truth wins out. Love never gives up, never loses faith, is always hopeful, and endures through every circumstance... There are three things that will endure—faith, hope, and love—and the greatest of these is love.
>
> —1 CORINTHIANS 13:1–7, 13

When we love others and obey the principles laid out in our Guide for life, it triggers a release of God's blessings. Obeying the Lord's simple request frequently serves as a springboard to our most extraordinary blessings. For example, in the following story, Simon Peter said yes to God, and a tremendous blessing came forth (Luke 5:1–11). One day a significant crowd pressed in around Jesus to listen to the Word of God. The Lord wanted to use Simon Peter's boat as a floating platform. He asked Simon Peter to push the boat a bit away from shore. Although Simon Peter was a professional fisherman, he did not question the sensibility of Jesus' directives. At times we might also receive instructions that do not appear reasonable. However, we must decide whether to follow human standards or obey God. Never allow human logic to deter you from obedience to God's plan. Simon Peter obeyed the request, and it paved his way into an extraordinary blessing.

When Jesus had finished speaking, He said to Simon Peter:

> "Now go out where it is deeper and let down your nets, and you will catch many fish." "Master," Simon replied, "we worked hard all last

night and didn't catch a thing. But if you say so, we'll try again." And this time their nets were so full they began to tear! A shout for help brought their partners in the other boat, and soon both boats were filled with fish and on the verge of sinking. When Simon Peter realized what had happened, he fell to his knees before Jesus and said, "Oh, Lord, please leave me—I'm too much of a sinner to be around you." For he was awestruck by the size of their catch, as were the others with him. His partners, James and John, the sons of Zebedee, were also amazed. Jesus replied to Simon Peter, "Don't be afraid! From now on you'll be fishing for people!" And as soon as they landed, they left everything and followed Jesus.

—Luke 5:4–11

God chooses ordinary people to do His work. The key is to listen for His voice and respond to the call. Only those who are listening will be tapped for an assignment. It is impossible to listen without knowing the voice. Get to know the voice of the Creator.

Prior to receiving this divinely discerned project, I had become a bit anxious. One Saturday afternoon while engaged in one of my conversations with God, I said, "God, this employment situation has dragged for so many years, and I am having anxiety attacks. Am I doing something outside of your will?" I received no response. I continued the conversation. I said, "God, the lottery is in the millions for this week, and I would like to buy a ticket." Again, no answer! I said, "God, if I am not to play, I need a sign." The next day at church, at the end of the sermon, the pastor said, "There was someone that requested a sign from God about the lottery. The answer is no. God is able to exceed the benefit of any lottery." The following evening I was led to read the below scripture, and it came up clear in my spirit that God is my Source, not the lottery.

No eye has seen, no ear has heard, and no mind has imagined what God has prepared for those who love him.

—1 Corinthians 2:9

About two months later my direction to write this book was not only divinely discerned, but my task was confirmed by several sources. God is no respecter of persons. What He does for one, He will do for all.

Consider these reasons why knowledge of the Word of God, faith coupled with obedience, is absolutely critical to a successful Christian life.

Obeying God in small matters is an essential step to God's greatest blessings.

Suppose I had said to God, "I need to find a job. I do not have time to write Your book." I would have been in complete disobedience and would not have been poised to receive the blessings I am now receiving. Had I said anything other than yes, I would have missed the greatest experience of my life. God's greatest blessing came because I trusted Him to be my Source, not an employer.

Our obedience always benefits others.

When we obey God, sharing what God is doing in our lives motivates us to tell others. This encourages others to trust Him and ultimately increases their faith. I believe that many people will be blessed because of my obedience. We must realize that God's Word has a solution for every peril we are confronted with.

Our obedience never leads to disappointment.

When we obey God, the outcome of our obedience is seldom disappointment. When I first confronted this task, I thought to myself, "I am no writer." But instead of following my personal thoughts I obeyed God, and His Spirit within me did the work. God spoke through me and used the Holy Spirit to develop my writing skills. Like Simon Peter, I realized that when it comes to the Creator of the universe there is no other safe option than to obey.

> And we know that God causes everything to work together for the good of those who love God and are called according to his purpose for them.
>
> —ROMANS 8:28

When we are ignorant to the Word of God, we are unaware of how we are led. If we do not know the Word faith cannot come, and therefore we are unable to obey.

INFANT BAPTISM

One of the areas where I believe we follow dogma and not God's Word is with infant baptism.

What is baptism?

Baptism, is "a ceremonial immersion in water, or application of water, as an initiatory rite or sacrament of the Christian church."[1] Baptism symbolizes the death, burial, and resurrection of the old, sinful ways to newness in

Christ. Many Christians often baptize or christen their babies as a ritual. However, this is not a ritual that is rooted in the Word of God.

Since an infant does not have the understanding to accept Jesus and since his parents cannot accept Jesus for him/her, the religious ritual of Christening is deceptive. In actuality, when we practice such a ritual, we are providing a false assurance of salvation to those who have never made a personal commitment to follow Jesus Christ. Baptism is a new believer's response to faith. It is a declaration that an individual has given their life to Jesus Christ. In order to do that, one must be capable of making such a decision, and infants are not. It is important that we teach the newness of light in God based on a relationship with Him and not religious activities. It is irresponsible on our part to continue to engage in the practice of religious rituals that have no basis in the Word of God. This is not to say we cannot pray for our children, dedicate them to Christ, or make our own promise to God to teach them the way of the Word. In fact, we should do this. However, as developed Christians, we should not perpetuate deceptive types of rituals in generations to come.

Jesus commissioned His followers to go make disciples: "Therefore, go and make disciples of all the nations, baptizing them in the name of the Father and the Son and the Holy Spirit" (Matt. 28:19).

The baptism of Jesus

Jesus began His public ministry with baptism. However, Jesus had no sin to repent. Unlike Jesus, the newly born come into the world with a sin nature. As Christians we are called to follow His lead in all things as we grow in our faith. Matthew 3:13–17 tells us this about Jesus' experience getting baptized:

> Then Jesus went from Galilee to the Jordan River to be baptized by John. But John didn't want to baptize him. "I am the one who needs to be baptized by you," he said, "so why are you coming to me?" But Jesus said, "It must be done, because we must do everything that is right." So then John baptized him. After his baptism, as Jesus came up out of the water, the heavens were opened and he saw the Spirit of God descending like a dove and settling on him. And a voice from heaven said, "This is my beloved Son, and I am fully pleased with him."

As parents and grandparents, it is important that we understand that baptism is not equivalent to salvation. Baptism is a symbolic way of expressing our faith. In the same manner in which the Lord conquered death and rose again, we are also spiritually resurrected into a new life when we believe.

We need to educate our young ones about the truth of the Word of God. The Word of God makes it very clear: a person's sins are forgiven based on belief in Christ rather than through baptism. Who should be baptized? Only those who have been saved by grace through faith in Jesus should be baptized. Baptism connects believers not only to Christ but also to our spiritual brothers and sisters, past, present, and future.

You Can Do This!

This phrase was my 2011 mantra once I received the assignment to write this book. I awoke one morning in July 2011 and prayed, "God, I do not know that I am able to do this. I can't write, do not feel qualified, and am clueless about what to say. And who would want to listen anyway?" I said to God, "I need more of You," and I meditated on this scripture to gain strength: "Don't be afraid, for I am with you. Don't be dismayed, for I am your God. I will strengthen you. I will help you. I will hold you up with my victorious right hand" (Isa. 41:10). Meditating on God's Word increased my faith and kept me connected to His Spirit within me. Once I became completely convinced that all the doing was coming from God, I focused and allowed the Holy Spirit to lead. The assignment then became feasible. The Spirit of God within me led this entire assignment.

The message to you is that God is no respecter of persons. He loves all of humanity with the same fervor as Jesus. He has an assignment for you. To receive the message you must believe, have faith, and accept Him as Lord of your life. Access to receive communication from His Spirit to yours begins with this first vital step. I challenge you to be courageous and step out in faith. There is a life in eternity at stake.

> The Holy Spirit says, "Today you must listen to his voice. Don't harden your hearts against him as Israel did when they rebelled, when they tested God's patience in the wilderness. There your ancestors tried my patience, even though they saw my miracles for forty years. So I was angry with them, and I said, 'Their hearts always turn away from me. They refuse to do what I tell them.' So in my anger I made a vow: 'They will never enter my place of rest.'"…Make sure that your own hearts are not evil and unbelieving, turning you away from the living God.
>
> —Hebrews 3:7–12

PART 4:
CHART YOUR PATHWAY INTO ETERNITY

Take a Stand in Your Journey

DISCOVER YOUR TRUE JOURNEY

OUR ATTENTION SPAN for the Word of God is determined by our yearning and our passion to know Him. Without opening the Guidebook, it is impossible to travel through this journey successfully. The intent of our journey was to be one of trust in the knowledge, power, and wisdom of God's Word, not in our own strength.

Everything that has ever been created in the earth's realm has been accomplished by a spoken word.

> In the beginning the Word already existed. He was with God, and he was God. He was in the beginning with God. He created everything there is. Nothing exists that he didn't make. Life itself was in him, and this life gives light to everyone. The light shines through the darkness, and the darkness can never extinguish it. God sent John the Baptist to tell everyone about the light so that everyone might believe because of his testimony. John himself was not the light; he was only a witness to the light. The one who is the true light, who gives light to everyone, was going to come into the world. But although the world was made through him, the world didn't recognize him when he came. Even in his own land and among his own people, he was not accepted. But to all who believed him and accepted him, he gave the right to become children of God. They are reborn! This is not a physical birth resulting from human passion or plan—this rebirth comes from God. So the Word became human and lived here on earth among us. He was full of unfailing love and faithfulness. And we have seen his glory, the glory of the only Son of the Father.
>
> —JOHN 1:1–14

We were predestined to live a journey with a playbook written by the Creator of the universe. However, many of us have rebelled against our Creator by ignoring the playbook and succumbing to the ineffective standards of the world system. Consequently, we have missed the steps to tap in to heavenly wisdom. We are so impressed with ourselves and caught up with the limitations of humanity that we are unable to grasp the big picture of our true purpose in this journey called life. Earthly intellect and egos, coupled with greed, have kept our society in subjugation. In spite of the fact that we claim life in a democracy, we are a society living in bondage—and many are too ignorant to recognize it.

Continued rebellion against our Creator will perpetuate ignorance. When people are aware of their ignorance and oppression, there is hope, but when they are not, they are destined for destruction. The society we live in has been many years in the making, and the inevitable outcome is the world as we see it today. Darkness! We have become a society of followers of the dictates of mere man. Until every person uncovers the true reason for his or her earthly existence, he or she will continue to be oppressed in their roles as followers.

> So Christ has really set us free. Now make sure that you stay free, and don't get tied up again in slavery to the law.
> —GALATIANS 5:1

The price of freedom was paid two thousand years ago by our Lord Jesus Christ. Yet, through our actions, it appears that many of us prefer darkness, bondage, and rebellion and have succumbed to that lifestyle. We are never truly free until we achieve freedom from the inside. Freedom is "exemption from external control, interference, [or] regulations... [It is] the power to determine action without restraint."[1] In order to free ourselves from the inside out, we must discover the reason why we were created. Complete freedom only comes from the Spirit of God within the believer who has accepted Jesus into their heart.

> For you have been called to live in freedom—not freedom to satisfy your sinful nature, but freedom to serve one another in love.
> —GALATIANS 5:13

Each day we walk through a journey making many choices. We are faced with hundreds of options and decisions to make that eventually lead us to the light or complete darkness. Whether we know it or not, we are always given the choice to follow God's way or our own. Those who are doers of God's Word will habitually forsake their own desires and embrace the Father's will. At times, the choices we are given involve simple decisions, and other times they are more complex, like the selection of a life partner.

The irony is that in the majority of instances, we do not consider the consequences of our decisions until after the fact. By then it is too late, and the consequences may create havoc in our lives.

There are several reasons why I believe we do not seek resources from the Bible. We lack faith, trust, and most importantly, the discipline to be obedient to the Word of God.

Nonetheless, God is not in the business of providing instant solutions to our problems that also might create an additional hindrance for us. To understand God's will for us requires time in the Word, which ultimately leads to direction and revelation. When we choose to use kingdom resources, we give God access to mold us so that gradually we might develop into the likeness of His Son. Over time, with meditation on the Word, we internalize the message and develop a foundation that provides us the confidence that the Word will do what it says.

God has a purpose coupled with a plan not only for believers but unbelievers as well. For the unbelievers, He will wait patiently until they are ready to join His kingdom. Although we experience much uncertainty, believers in Christ have an extraordinary assurance that God always provides an outcome that leads to our maximum benefit. We get ourselves into trouble when we move without Him. However, in grace He is always willing to help when we ask.

> And we know that God causes everything to work together for the good of those who love God and are called according to his purpose for them.
>
> —Romans 8:28

It is extremely important that we all find our spiritual calling in life. God is the only One who is certain to get us there, for He devised a plan way before we came into existence. We are free to discover our own plan, or we can choose the surest road, His plan. To have a great career, great education, great income, and all else that one desires is grand. However, nothing is more extraordinary than adhering to a call from the Lord.

Keep in mind that we all are called in some form or fashion, but unfortunately only a few listen and respond. In order to discover the call it is important that we are in close fellowship with the One who calls. How do we do this? We study the Word of God. The call is not always easy to discover, and to pursue it requires faith. God requires absolute loyalty once we discern His divine assignment. If we allow it, He brings us to a point of total and complete dependence on Him, which is the ultimate response to the call. We must understand with complete confidence that what the Word states will be done.

I realized my spiritual shortcomings when I was stripped from what I considered to be security and consistency in income from employers. Not realizing it, many of us make our employers our god, and when we lose that income we fall into complete despondence. Most employees have never conceived that an employer might not be able to keep their commitment. What would you do if you were with a company for thirty or forty years, only to discover at retirement that the company was unable to pay those benefits you worked all your life for? We have given mere man too much authority over our lives and have completely disregarded the promises given by our Creator.

Many in the Earth's realm are in complete ignorance to their true Source, including those in the Christian community. Mere man will never be able to solve the world's needs. It is very unfortunate that a discovery of this magnitude usually only happens during periods when we have had an experience with adversity.

> Through suffering, these bodies of ours constantly share in the death of Jesus so that the life of Jesus may also be seen in our bodies.
> —2 CORINTHIANS 4:10

Had I not gone through the extended period of unemployment, I am not certain that I would have received this revelation so clearly.

> When people do not accept divine guidance, they run wild. But whoever obeys the law is happy.
> —PROVERBS 29:18

Joy came for me as I pursued God and gradually discovered His ways. In order to truly know God we need to study His Word. God's promises are all set forth in the Bible. However, we either consider the guide unimportant or are reluctant to give it attention. It behooves us to refrain from leaving our eternal future in the hands of pastors, priests, and rabbis. It is our responsibility to educate ourselves concerning the laws of the kingdom of God. The discovery is comparable to being awakened from unconsciousness. It is as if a light bulb comes on in the darkness. It is the joy and wonder of being told, "I have already paid your sin debt in full. Wake up and receive the gift. It is free."

> The Spirit is God's guarantee that he will give us everything he promised and that he has purchased us to be his own people. This is just one more reason for us to praise our glorious God.
>
> —Ephesians 1:14

Everything has been given to us—health, wealth, and abundance in every area of life. All that God requires of us is to read the directions and do what they say. For me, as I read and saw, I changed my behavior and aligned myself with the message. There is no halfway with God; either you are on board with the kingdom constitution, or you continue to follow your uncontrolled behavior in the world. It is all by choice, and it is up to you.

I was blessed when I discerned the call of this assignment. I felt completely renewed, not from doing something for my specific purpose but from receiving revelation from the will of God. We all are God's chosen. Unfortunately all too often we are unaware of a call; hence, we cannot hear it. During all my life experiences and relationships, none have ever rejuvenated my heart as this one has. Have you received an assignment from the Lord? If so, it is imperative that you commit and fulfill the assignment.

In my case, fear initially crept in to say, Who do you think you are? However, when you have an overflow of God's Word within your spirit, it removes all the fear, and it becomes very easy to pull out the weapon, the sword of the Spirit, the Word of God. He tells us!

> Don't be afraid, for I am with you. Do not be dismayed, for I am your God. I will strengthen you. I will help you. I will uphold you with my victorious right hand.
>
> —Isaiah 41:10

Can you think of anyone in the Earth's realm that can offer this assurance? Anything we accomplish for God has a purpose beyond this life.

Wealth Does Not Equal Success

> The rich think of their wealth as an impregnable defense; they imagine it is a high wall of safety.
>
> —Proverbs 18:11

Many equate wealth with success. However, God measures success by the difference we make for His kingdom. Develop the relationship with Him, have faith, obey, and listen for His call. We were all predestined to play a part, have an assignment to accomplish His will for humanity. Therefore, we need to listen for the voice and the call. We learn the voice when we have the relationship with Him.

> But people who long to be rich fall into temptation and are trapped by many foolish and harmful desires that plunge them into ruin and destruction.
>
> —1 TIMOTHY 6:9

Do not make money your God. I must admit, before I received the entire revelation of truth in God, I was in ignorance to a fallacy that money was the solution to most problems. However, as I grew and developed in spiritual matters, I realized that money, without God, is useless. It is like a time bomb just waiting to explode. What comes to mind here is the entertainment industry, specifically Hollywood. Celebrities accumulate a mass amount of wealth, and this becomes the god for many of them. However, just take a peek at the destructive lifestyle the so-called rich and famous live. Many of their lives are dysfunctional, with much unhappiness and ignorance to the real purpose of our earthly existence. Financial success in the absence of the wisdom of God is short lived and a very temporal state of being.

THE FUTILITY OF PLEASURE

Pleasure is magnificent. However, there is emptiness that surfaces from living for oneself without ever considering the needs of others. Enlightenment concerning wisdom from above changes one's perspective regarding the reason for our earthly existence.

> For the greater my wisdom, the greater my grief. To increase knowledge only increases sorrow.
>
> —ECCLESIASTES 1:18

When one becomes enlightened concerning the reason God created humanity, it becomes impossible to just sit back and not share the discovery. Although it is the most valuable information to share with humanity, those of us who have experienced that burst of light from God are viewed as fanatics, and some might be forced not to share it.

Our world defines *wisdom* as using the knowledge we have gained rightly. Having godly wisdom means that we have the capability to see things from God's perspective and respond according to kingdom principles outlined in the Word. How do we acquire wisdom? Would you consider yourself a wise person?

> There is a path before each person that seems right, but it ends in death.
> —PROVERBS 16:25

Wisdom is a gift from God, and it behooves us to pursue it. Do not take for granted that the path you are on is the correct one. Eternity is a heartbeat away. Make sure the path you are on is the right one. During my discovery process, I had the most extraordinary epiphany that my life's battle was already fought and won by our Creator. Our part is to adhere to His direction, given by way of the Holy Spirit, and apply it in our life.

Personally, when I came to this place I said, "God, I know my heart's desires. However, if my desires do not align with Yours, I am prepared to let them go." This is when everything changed for me. The peace of God, which surpasses all understanding, came over me, and it has remained to this date. I received the message of truth loud and clear. It is not an easy journey, but it is the surest of all other alternatives.

Humanity is full of highly educated and successful people. However, many of those people are so dissatisfied with their lives that they have become involved in self-destructive behavior such as drugs, alcohol, addictions, and other abusive behavior patterns. Why is this? The major reason is inflated egos, coupled with the pursuit of limitless pleasures and what the material world defines as success. However, without wisdom from above, our life ultimately turns to ashes. In the absence of a relationship with our Creator, all accomplishments, no matter how great, lead to continued feelings of incompletion.

King Solomon was a perfect demonstration of this. (See 1 Kings 11). Here you have a king who has been identified as the wisest man who ever lived. He was blessed with wealth beyond his wildest dreams and bestowed with the honor to build God's temple. Think about what a privilege it must have been to be in relationship with the Creator of the universe. Why was he so wise? He asked for wisdom, and it was granted. Many of us ask God for things when we pray. Primarily, Solomon was smart enough to know that there was more to life than riches.

However, Solomon indulged in world's pleasures—he pursued foolish things, had many wives, and engaged in idol worship—and still he was unable to experience true happiness. Why is that? We were created to be in intimate, personal relationship with our Creator. In the absence of that relationship our heart will always be unfulfilled and in longing for Him. Solomon lost focus, disobeyed God, and married foreign women, which led him to worship other gods. The satisfaction Solomon pursued evaded him, and he realized that self-indulgence was absolutely insignificant. Solomon discovered the emptiness of living and pleasing self. He involved himself in so many ways; he improved the environment with garden parks and extensive irrigation projects. He accumulated more wealth than man would ever want or need. However, in the end he found it all without meaning.

> I said to myself, "Come now, let's give pleasure a try. Let's look for the 'good things' in life." But I found that this, too, was meaningless. "It is silly to be laughing all the time," I said. "What good does it do to seek only pleasure?" After much thought, I decided to cheer myself with wine. While still seeking wisdom, I clutched at foolishness. In this way, I hoped to experience the only happiness most people find during their brief life in this world. I also tried to find meaning by building huge homes for myself and by planting beautiful vineyards. I made gardens and parks, filling them with all kinds of fruit trees. I built reservoirs to collect the water to irrigate my many flourishing groves. I bought slaves, both men and women, and others were born into my household. I also owned great herds and flocks, more than any of the kings who lived in Jerusalem before me. I collected great sums of silver and gold, the treasure of many kings and provinces. I hired wonderful singers, both men and women, and had many beautiful concubines. I had everything a man could desire! So I became greater than any of the kings who ruled in Jerusalem before me. And with it all, I remained clear-eyed so that I could evaluate all these things. Anything I wanted, I took. I did not restrain myself from any joy. I even found great pleasure in hard work, an additional reward for all my labors. But as I looked at everything I had worked so hard to accomplish, it was all so meaningless. It was like chasing the wind. There was nothing really worthwhile anywhere.
> —ECCLESIASTES 2:1–11

King Solomon was given godly wisdom and all the resources imaginable. However, he was consumed with earthly and short-lived objectives, instant gratification, and matters involving idle worship, which in the long run, destroyed his kingdom. Solomon disconnected from God's positioning system (GPS). At the end, he concluded that the best course was to obey

God. A lesson for humanity today is this: All that is acquired outside the will of God eventually turns to ashes, as Solomon's kingdom did.

Are you connected to God's positioning system? Who is your god? Who are you obeying? The fall of a once strong and mighty believer in God does not take place overnight. It is usually a result of choices over a period of time that are completely unaligned with God's Word.

The Unfolding Revelation

When the Lord invited me to follow Him, I surrendered all else to pursue a new identity in Him. During the experience of enlightenment, I realized that nothing on Earth was more important than this discovery. My experience was very humbling. It began with changes in my professional life, which included a decrease in both my salary and position. My salary was no longer the six figures to which I had grown accustomed. Additionally, I moved from an executive-level to an administrative-level position. However, my objective now is very different from what it was prior to my commitment to the kingdom. Now I am not just working a job; I am on assignment for the kingdom of God. I will adhere to the mandate that accompanies my assignment until my heavenly Father releases me from this position. I have yet to see the entire picture. However, I am also aware that in God's omnipotence, He has all the power to reach the audience He wants to with this work. He knows the final destination of this assignment, and I have absolute faith and trust that He will reveal it in His time.

For as long as I can remember prior to my enlightenment, I had put all of my trust in mere man, and the outcome was nowhere close to the extraordinary achievements I have always had in my heart. I have now decided to rely only on the great I Am to lead me every step of the rest of my journey. When I committed and started to develop an intimate, personal relationship with our Father, the Creator of the universe, by way of His Word, revelation came forth. I had no idea of what I was about to step into. I never envisioned the pursuit would require giving up close relationships. The relationships I speak of are those in our lives that hinder our walk with God. When the Spirit of God revealed the ones that hindered my walk, I was prudent and released them immediately. For me personally, there were a couple of them. Basically, I did not have to do anything. God just removed the relationships supernaturally. All we need to do is surrender and give God free range.

I also did not anticipate an extended season of heartaches, setbacks, and a stream of continuous perils, one after the other. My unemployment saga continued for a period of seven years. I believed it was divinely timed and aligned with my available personal income. I was forced to exhaust personal savings so that I might be in complete dependence on Him. By power of the spirit within, I was thrust into that complete surrender and dependency of God for complete sustenance. Ultimately, unemployment was the greatest blessing I have ever experienced in my life. Presently they are millions of people unemployed. Some are looking to the government, politicians, or employers for a fix. I say this from experience: Neither have the power to fix the problem. Take your problem to the real Source. He is the Creator and Fixer of all things. If our leaders were looking to the great I Am for solutions, the world would not be in the chaos that it is in today. Get your belief system right. The true Source of all in the Earth's realm is the Creator of the universe.

Spiritual discovery eludes many in the Christian community and in churches around the world. Why? Many in the body of Christ confront adversities only with the guidance and direction of mere man. However, they would never conceive of a total dependence of God for complete sustenance. I was told by a Christian in my church, "The Lord helps those who help themselves." That person was obviously accustomed to solving problems according to his own strength and considered it a waste of time to call on God. I believe that person could not conceive of the idea of the Bible as a resource during adversity. He had not considered that I was doing exactly what the Lord wanted. I was actively doing all the due diligence required and at the same time was looking to Him, believing, and having faith in the Word. It becomes very difficult, if not impossible, to explain the reasoning behind using the Bible as a resource for solutions to perils.

During this journey, I discovered a kingdom ironically unknown to many Christians and unbelievers, a realm beyond my wildest expectation. This experience has brought me to the realization that one word, one promise, from God is powerful enough to change a life forever. It is very difficult to explain. With God things happen supernaturally: "Just as you can hear the wind but can't tell where it comes from or where it is going, so you can't explain how people are born of the Spirit" (John 3:8).

My suggestion to both believers and non-believers is to get in the Word of God before it's too late. Do not fail to notice an extraordinary opportunity of an open door that leads to eternity. Humbly ask the great I Am, and He will give you direction.

As my relationship with Him developed, I realized that as long as I do my part, God will never break His covenant promise, outlined in the Bible. Promises are given to us; however, we do not receive them until we have developed enough to understand them. Think of how we release gifts to our children. Would you purchase an automobile for your child before they received a driver's license? No, because that would be irresponsible. It works the same with God. If He gave us gifts that we were not mature enough to receive, we would self-destruct.

Up until ten years ago I was consistent in church attendance, like most Christians. However, I neglected to take time to read the Word of God. Big mistake! Like many Christians, I spent a lot of years living in ignorance because I did not pay attention to the number one resource provided. Are you visiting a church dwelling weekly and still in ignorance to the Word of God? It is extremely important to take the time to address this question. If you are living in ignorance to God, make the correction today. The decision you make today will impact your eternal life.

BE GRATEFUL FOR PERILS

When adversity hits you from all areas, do not allow it to take you into hopelessness. Instead, think of it as an opportunity that God allowed into your life to stimulate your spiritual growth. Without overcoming perils in life, we remain stagnant and undeveloped. Our struggles never catch God by surprise. He allows them so that He might use the experience to accomplish His perfect will in our life. God in His omniscience sees what is coming before it gets to us. When we go to Him in prayer for help, He requires that we trust, have faith, obey, and leave the outcome to Him.

Had I not experienced adversity, I would have most likely continued in a state of spiritual ignorance. Make no mistake: a commitment to follow God does not mean we no longer experience adversity. In fact, the perilous conditions sometimes escalate with our commitment. Why? Whenever we discover the security that comes from a relationship with God, adversaries will attack. The attack comes because we have independently disconnected ourselves from the world's ignorant and rebellious ways, ways against those things connected to the kingdom of God. The devil will then try to steer us away from the journey with God. In my case, the attack came when I made a commitment to adhere to a call from God. Whenever we set out to accomplish something extraordinary and good in God, the adversary will always appear with some form of temptation. In the past ten years of my life I have experienced more adversity than at previous times during my life. They all commenced when I committed to make God's Word the final authority in my life.

If our usual reaction to difficulties is to play the victim, get angry, or become depressed, then the idea of experiencing tranquility during negative situations might not appear rational. However, if we dig deep within ourselves, we will discover that the biblical directives make absolute sense. Our primary reaction to pain is to resort to a Band-Aid fix or an instant, feel-good pill. However, God's objective is to teach us endurance so that we might benefit from the newness He is working out within our heart. When we realize that adversity is the salve that contributes to our completeness, we will change our outlook on struggles. While a worldly viewpoint would consider this approach naïve, spiritually we're succeeding on a journey to life at its fullest.

ADDITIONAL INSIGHT

The moment we begin to understand the truth of who God is, who we are in Him, we are equipped to be fruitful and productive servants for the kingdom. This journey is bigger than us. It is about God's will for humanity. In order to undertake the objective we need to fix our inner being so that we might present the best outer being. Personally, I had been seeking this truth all of my life, but was just not aware of how to find it. I had no idea that the grace of God would ever consider little me for one of His assignments. This is the absolute ultimate revelation. It is greater than winning an Academy Award, an Olympic gold medal, and even beyond having a net worth of a billion dollars. None of these could ever come close to the inner joy and peace that comes from the experience of a personal, intimate relationship with the Creator of the universe.

> Tell those who are rich in this world not to be proud and not to trust
> in their money, which will soon be gone. But their trust should be
> in the living God, who richly gives us all we need for our enjoyment.
> —1 TIMOTHY 6:17

Life is a journey, and who we choose to follow will determine the outcome. When we follow the world way in ignorance and rebellion to God, our outcome is very short-lived success. When we align our thinking with the kingdom of God, we will experience godly wisdom and eternal success. My personal and ultimate objective at this juncture in my journey would be to have our Creator say, "Well done, good and faithful servant!"

> The master said, "Well done, my good and faithful servant. You
> have been faithful in handling this small amount, so now I will
> give you many more responsibilities. Let's celebrate together!"
> —MATTHEW 25:23

While still in the Earth's realm, my objective is to leave my daughter with a legacy of the Word of God. My expectations are that she will in turn carry on the legacy for generations to follow. There is no greater gift that a parent could bestow on a child than to follow the guide given and imitate the steps given by our Creator. If believers in the body of Christ were able to drill down the message to listen to God and make His Word their final authority, that would be enough wisdom to entice unbelievers to not only pursue God but also to emulate Him.

Make loving your fellow man your number one priority. Develop a listening heart, and expect to hear from God. If I am able to play only a minuscule part in spreading this Word, I consider myself honored and blessed for having received the assignment. Nothing in this life will ever top an assignment from God.

My prayer for you is that you will seek God's wisdom during your perils and keep your eyes on the Source of all good things. My desire for every person who reads this book is that the message will sink so deeply in your hearts that you will be compelled to share it.

> Ever since I first heard of your strong faith in the Lord Jesus and your love for Christians everywhere, I have never stopped thanking God for you. I pray for you constantly, asking God, the glorious Father of our Lord Jesus Christ, to give you spiritual wisdom and understanding, so that you might grow in your knowledge of God. I pray that your hearts will be flooded with light so that you can understand the wonderful future he has promised to those he called. I want you to realize what a rich and glorious inheritance he has given to his people. I pray that you will begin to understand the incredible greatness of his power for us who believe him. This is the same mighty power that raised Christ from the dead and seated him in the place of honor at God's right hand in the heavenly realms. Now he is far above any ruler or authority or power or leader or anything else in this world or in the world to come. And God has put all things under the authority of Christ, and he gave him this authority for the benefit of the church. And the church is his body; it is filled by Christ, who fills everything everywhere with his presence.
>
> —Ephesians 1:15–23

THE FINAL DESTINATION

People's faces were austere in utter terror. They all had expressions of despondence and fear. They had been having too much fun and never gave a serious thought to that final destination. They had not considered life's most important activity, listening to God to receive direction.

This is what people likely experienced when God flooded the Earth to rid it of all the evil and wickedness His people created. There was one righteous man among all the people, Noah, who found favor in God's eyes. Noah was a type, a shadow, of the Jesus to come. God gave Noah some specific instructions. He told him to build an ark so that his entire family might be spared from the catastrophic disaster that was about to consume the Earth's entire population. Noah was also instructed to "take along seven pairs of each animal that I have approved for eating and for sacrifice, and take one pair of each of the others" (Gen. 7:2). Just imagine if God had given you these instructions. Visualize what Noah's neighbors might have thought as they observed him building this ark. Most likely they believed that he was a strange one or perhaps losing his mind. What would you have done? Do you believe that if God gave you instructions today you would know that He was speaking to you? Would you obey His instructions in spite of criticism from others? I believe that in order to adhere to directions from God, it is necessary to know Him, which is accomplished by reading His Word. Noah's obedience resulted in the blessing of continued earthly life for him, his family, and all the animals he was instructed to take. The rest of Earth's population chose to remain in rebellion and unawareness about what was to happen.

Rain fell on the entire Earth's population for a period of forty days and nights, and the flooding wiped out the entire face of the Earth with the exception of Noah, his family, and the animals he brought on the ark. Although God promised, "I solemnly promise never to send another flood to kill all living creatures and destroy the earth" (Gen. 9:11), humanity continues to self-destruct and blame God for it.

> My people are being destroyed because they don't know me. It is all your fault, you priests, for you yourselves refuse to know me. Now I refuse to recognize you as my priests. Since you have forgotten the laws of your God, I will forget to bless your children.
>
> —HOSEA 4:6

What is interesting about the Flood is that while Noah and his family prepared for a disastrous situation, as wise people do, the rest of humanity was busy having fun and were oblivious to what was about to occur. This is similar to the current state of our society. We are headed down the same ruinous path as the people back then. When Noah, his family, and others who God permitted to be a part of the journey entered the ark, the rest of the population was unaware of the fact that their final destination was upon them. This destiny is inescapable, so it behooves us to consider where we will spend eternity.

The moment we were born, the clock started ticking towards our final destination. Many of us have given little thought to how our actions in the Earth's realm impact eternity. With each day we are inching closer to that predestined appointment. It is the time when we will stand before our holy God to be judged or rewarded for the lives we have led. There is absolutely nothing that will exempt us from this appointment.

> Our days on earth are like grass; like wildflowers, we bloom and die. The wind blows, and we are gone—as though we had never been here. But the love of the Lord remains forever with those who fear him. His salvation extends to the children's children of those who are faithful to his covenant, of those who obey his commandments!
> —Psalm 103:15–18

It is very interesting how the human mind works. For the majority of us it takes adversity for God to get our attention. At times, even with difficulties, we still do not get it. Instead, we turn to the wicked ways of the world for an instant fix as a solution to our troubles. We were given God's Word to allow us to carry on in the wise way. God operates today the same way as He did in the days of Noah. As a believer, it is possible to find the same favor as Noah did with God. Read the Word and walk with God in an intimate, personal relationship, and you will have favor. Obey God even though His request sometimes appears to be unreasonable.

Whenever Jesus began a story about sowing seeds, He always finished with a harvest. For example, the Word of God is a seed to be planted in our heart, and it works in the same manner as when a farmer plants seeds into the ground. A farmer receives his harvest based on the soil and all the other strategies used in farming. The Word of God will produce a harvest like the farmer. In this parable, the seed is the Word of God, the soil is our heart, and the process is as follows:

> The seed is God's message. The seed that fell on the hard path represents those who hear the message, but then the Devil comes and steals it away and prevents them from believing and being saved.

The rocky soil represents those who hear the message with joy. But like young plants in such soil, their roots don't go very deep. They believe for a while, but they wilt when the hot winds of testing blow. The thorny ground represents those who hear and accept the message, but all too quickly the message is crowded out by the cares and riches and pleasures of this life. And so they never grow into maturity. But the good soil represents honest, good-hearted people who hear God's message, cling to it, and steadily produce a huge harvest.

—LUKE 8:11–15

The takeaway from Jesus' lessons was always for us to understand that whatever we do in the Earth's realm will create an end result in the heavenly realm. Like it or not, financial status, job title, authority level, educational level, friends, associates, or family we have in high places will not exempt us from this encounter. Are you prepared?

The sun will be turned into darkness, and the moon will turn blood red before that great and terrible day of the LORD arrives.

—JOEL 2:31

In His omniscience, God is the only one privy to the end result in our lives. If you were to focus on your final destination, what would you do? What things would you eliminate from your life? You might even say, "Why would I care about that? I am just interested in having fun and enjoying life now." Despite popular belief, our last breath in the Earth's realm may be taken at any second, minute, or hour. Without focus on eternity or preparation to meet our Maker, many of us are living life recklessly. We have been given the choice of where we will spend eternity—heaven or hell. "How do you know there is a heaven or a hell?" you ask. The answer to that question can be the topic of an entirely new book. In the meantime, hopefully you do not want to die unsaved to confirm the accuracy of whether or not hell exists.

Today I have given you the choice between life and death, between blessings and curses. I call on heaven and earth to witness the choice you make. Oh, that you would choose life, that you and your descendants might live! Choose to love the LORD your God and to obey him and commit yourself to him, for he is your life. Then you will live long in the land the LORD swore to give your ancestors Abraham, Isaac, and Jacob.

—DEUTERONOMY 30:19–20

During the past few years I have had the opportunity to spend time in nursing homes and hospitals visiting with both Christians and non-believers in their sixty-plus years of existence. In spite of the fact that many have been Christians and in churches for thirty and forty years, the truly amazing thing is that so many of them have not taken the time to read the Word of God and don't have personal relationships with Him. Imagine living a lifetime on Earth going to church weekly without ever getting a revelation of who you are in Christ. This scenario accurately describes much of the body of Christ today. At this juncture, our world's population is in a sad place. In spite of all the resources at our disposal, much of humanity is preoccupied with instant gratification.

During one of my visits, I asked a woman, "When was the last time you read a Bible scripture?" She responded, "The Bible has been at my nightstand for thirty years." Only ten years ago did I myself pick it up and read it, the entire book. You may have just thought to yourself after reading this, "When was the last time I picked up the Bible?" or "What might I do differently, so that I can develop my relationship with my Creator?" Take heed. Time is running out. If your life were to end abruptly today, would you be prepared to meet your Maker? Would it not be sad to return to our Creator with the same level of ignorance in which He released us into the universe? That would be quite tragic! Are you in the know of the truth and light of God? Now is the time to prepare for the final destination.

A Society of Self-Directed People

We live in a society where people honor man more than they fear God. Many steer clear of offending anyone, yet they don't take exception to offending God. Many of us are afraid to stand up for the gospel, because it is not considered politically correct. I believe the reason we do not defend it is because many are not aware of the real message.

> How happy are those who fear the Lord—all who follow his ways! You will enjoy the fruit of your labor. How happy you will be! How rich your life! Your wife will be like a fruitful vine, flourishing within your home. And look at all those children! There they sit around your table as vigorous and healthy as young olive trees. That is the Lord's reward for those who fear him.
> —Psalm 128:1–4

Excellence in the world's way does not equate to excellence in God's standards of distinction. Academic education is necessary and important to live a life in the Earth's realm. However, when we live without the most important education of all, the Word of God, we have chosen to ignore the instructions provided by our Creator. It is impossible for us to know the road that will lead to the most successful outcome better than the One who knows the beginning, middle, and end. Although God created all things, He is the last person many would ever approach for counsel. Would you not like to have our omniscient God directing your steps?

The extraordinary thing about God's kingdom is its mission of justice and righteousness for all, which is a complete contrast to the wicked ways of the world we live in.

As in water face reflects face, So a man's heart reveals the man.
—PROVERBS 27:19, NKJV

Our earthly life is very short compared to the eternal Jesus offers. Unless you are working on assignment from God to accommodate His will for humanity, seemingly distinguished resumes, educational levels, professional positions, and other worldly credentials we strive to acquire will not lead to a successful kingdom destination. Humanity is so caught up with knowing the right people, with the right social connections, that the true purpose of life eludes many of us. Most of us are more interested in knowing wealthy people or amassing wealth, than knowing God or accumulating knowledge about God. Unfortunately, none of these frivolous earthly desires will provide us with access into the heavenly realm. What does it do to finish well in the affairs of the world, but in the end lose your soul? Salvation is the key to partake in eternity. Every good thing that comes to us is from God. This means that when we are placed in positions of authority, God expects us to carry out the mission in a righteous manner.

The story of Moses is a clear warning that God hates any form of injustice from any level of authority in our society. When God called Moses and gave him the assignment to free the Israelites from Egyptian bondage, it was a demonstration that He abhors injustice. Moses was born Hebrew. However, Pharaoh's daughter reared him as an Egyptian. Moses had the opportunity to live a life in the environment in which he grew up and became accustomed. However, his distaste for injustice led him to a higher calling (Exod. 3). I believe that was the reason God gave him the assignment to free the Israelites. From my study of the Word, I believe God looks at the heart and sees those things that we are passionate about, then assigns our path based on His will for humanity.

Pharaoh was the king of Egypt. When Moses entered Pharaoh's courtroom to give him the message from God, Pharaoh did not believe a higher authority existed other than himself, a "god on Earth." Likewise, there are many today in levels of authority that share Pharaoh's sentiment. Pharaoh defied the God of Abraham, Isaac, and Jacob. He refused to heed His command to let the Israelites go. Eventually he created destruction for himself and the Egyptians who were under his authority. The Lord bid all leaders in levels of authority to manage with the utmost of integrity. Biblical stories are not fairytales; they are historical and prophetic. Pharaoh was like many of today's taskmasters in the earthly realm. Once we obtain a certain level of earthly authority, arrogance, greed, and self-righteousness set in—until the wrath of God comes. God demonstrated His power over evil by defeating the enemies of the Hebrew people, and He will do the same today.

Those who have been placed in positions of authority should use their positions wisely, for, be assured, judgment is for all. God is interested in the use of godly wisdom to lead in any area where He appoints us. Just leadership only comes with the awareness of truth and fear of the Lord.

> A ruler who lacks understanding is a great oppressor, But he who hates covetousness will prolong his days.
> —PROVERBS 28:16, NKJV

Are you presently in a position of authority? I challenge you this moment to reflect on the level of integrity with which you lead! There are no special privileges given in the kingdom for those in opulent positions of power, education, or financial levels. Here is a word of wisdom for us all:

> Then if my people who are called by my name will humble themselves and pray and seek my face and turn from their wicked ways, I will hear from heaven and will forgive their sins and heal their land. I will listen to every prayer made in this place.
> —2 CHRONICLES 7:14–15

> Pride goes before destruction, and haughtiness before a fall.
> —PROVERBS 16:18

Take heed. Your last day in the Earth's realm might be today. Lead the way God predestined: with righteousness and justice to all who fall under your realm of responsibility.

CHOOSE CORRECTLY

World creation is an expression of God's divine, infinite, extraordinary power in both the heavenly and earthly realm. The truth of God's Word is the basic foundation for life. Humanity serves many gods, so why is Jesus the supreme God? For starters, God is love! He doesn't just have love; He is love.

> But anyone who does not love does not know God—for God is love.
> —1 JOHN 4:8

Love causes no harm to others. Are you able to experience unconditional love from the god you serve? Only the love of God defeats death. There is nothing that His love cannot conquer. It has no limit to its faith, hope, and endurance. Christianity is the only religion based on faith in Jesus Christ. All others are centered on performance.

> For there is only one God and one Mediator who can reconcile God and people. He is the man Christ Jesus.
> —1 TIMOTHY 2:5

What other god has died and been resurrected by the power of the Holy Spirit? Are you able to develop an intimate relationship with the god you serve? If you are serving a god who is no longer in existence or one unable to provide inner wisdom, direction, and spiritual guidance, that behavior is called idol worship. The conduct equates to the worship of a powerless, deceased person who neither has authority in the Earth nor in the kingdom realm. The benefits you derive from God should be visibly displayed in the way you live. The choice you make now determines your eternal destiny.

> Christ is the visible image of the invisible God. He existed before God made anything at all and is supreme over all creation.
> —COLOSSIANS 1:15

When we make Jesus the Lord of our lives, God is our Father. Jesus is the only God that is not manmade and has his origins in the Spirit of the Creator of the universe. Think about it! Other faiths have prophets that have died. However, Jesus is the only One who has risen from the dead and continues with life. Who is your god or idol?

> You cannot drink from the cup of the Lord and from the cup of demons, too. You cannot eat at the Lord's Table and at the table of demons, too.
> —1 Corinthians 10:21

The Creator of the universe is the only God that has provided the following assurance. Jesus said:

> Don't be troubled. You trust God, now trust in me. There are many rooms in my Father's home, and I am going to prepare a place for you. If this were not so, I would tell you plainly. When everything is ready, I will come and get you, so that you will always be with me where I am. And you know where I am going and how to get there.
> —John 14:1–4

There is no other god or prophet that has ever guaranteed a place in eternity other than the God of Abraham, Isaac, and Jacob. The Word of God is the Source of all life, and this life brought light to all people (John 1).

The journey ends when we take our last breath. Jesus is our end result and final destination. When we adhere to other belief systems that exclude Jesus Christ, it will exclude us from a final destination in the heavenly kingdom of God. Prepare yourself and do not delay!

The Preordained Appointment

How do we prepare for our final destination? The alignment of God's Word to our daily activity is the most assured way to reach the end result. Have faith in God. Faith begins when we know the will of God. It is impossible to have faith without knowing God's will, His Word.

> What is faith? It is the confident assurance that what we hope for is going to happen. It is the evidence of things we cannot yet see. God gave his approval to people in days of old because of their faith.
> —Hebrews 11:1–2

The story of Joshua during the time he was Moses' assistant was a great display of how faith is developed. Although there was no written Bible back then, the Israelites were able to see God's power through His deeds. The

Israelites had an opportunity to experience firsthand God's protection to His people. When God brought His people out of Egypt He said, "On that night I will pass through the land of Egypt and kill all the firstborn sons and firstborn male animals in the land of Egypt. I will execute judgment against all the gods of Egypt, for I am the LORD! The blood you have smeared on your doorposts will serve as a sign. When I see the blood, I will pass over you. This plague of death will not touch you when I strike the land of Egypt" (Exod. 12:12–13). Later, the parting of the Red Sea, which allowed the Israelites to cross the water on dry land, was a great demonstration of God's power. On the banks of the sea Moses told the people:

> Don't be afraid. Just stand where you are and watch the LORD rescue you. The Egyptians that you see today will never be seen again. The LORD himself will fight for you. You won't have to lift a finger in your defense!
>   —EXODUS 14:13–14

Did you know that God does the same for believers today? Today, although often we do not witness God's deeds in quite the same way, we get a glimpse of how God operates by reading His words. And when we really get in tune with His Spirit, we also are able to witness His deeds firsthand.

A few years ago God showed me a display of His power. I had an experience with a legal situation where a frivolous lawsuit was brought against me. When I received notice of a court date, the Spirit of God told me exactly what to do. He said, "I am your Source. Do not get an attorney. Go to court, and I will give you instructions. Get to court early. When you get in the courtroom, sit in the back. Do not speak unless my Spirit says." When the case was called, the attorney for the plaintiff got up and said, "Ready." I had spoken to the attorney on the phone; however, the first time I actually saw him was when he responded to the roll call. I adhered to God's direction in obedience. I simply obeyed. I sat in the back of the court room and read while I waited. About forty-five minutes later the case was called, and the attorney got up again and said, "Your honor, this case was settled." I kid you not! The judge instructed the clerk to record the case dismissed. As I was about to go over to the attorney, the Spirit of God stopped me and said, "It is finished. Go home." It was one of the most awesome experiences, and I have had so many of these extraordinary displays of God's power and favor in my life. One of the most powerful blessings in the Earth's realm is to know your Source, abide in Him, have faith in Him, trust Him, obey Him, and allow Him to become responsible for your end result.

For those unfamiliar with the story of Moses, after his death, the leadership of the nation passed into the hands of Joshua. He was one of the twelve spies who went into the Promised Land and was not afraid to possess the land. However, there were ten others who were afraid. Joshua's faith was very developed, and he was willing to do anything God instructed him to do. He had seen God's awesome power in the past and trusted Him. Because of faith, trust, and obedience in God, Joshua led the children of Israel into the Promised Land (Josh. 1–4). God is looking for believers to know Him intimately, like Joshua, so that He might display the same power He displayed then.

How do we get faith? Faith is a phenomenon beyond the human comprehension. It supernaturally comes when we repeatedly listen to and focus on God's Word. Scripture tells us "faith comes by hearing, and hearing by the word of God" (Rom. 10:17, NKJV).

What can hinder our faith and prevent us from successfully reaching our destiny? Ignorance of God's Word, lack of faith, or perhaps no faith at all! Would you consider transferring the faith you have in the world's system and placing it in the hands of our Creator? Removing our trust from the world and putting it in God will result in the extraordinary. There are those who might say, "I have already accomplished the extraordinary. I am wealthy and able to buy anything and do all that I want." That is all well and good. However, there is a slight problem with this type of reasoning. Without acceptance of Jesus as Lord, a life in eternity is not possible. When we only have faith in mere man, we relinquish our opportunity for a life in eternity. After all, Jesus is the key to open that door.

Hindrances to Our Faith

Lack of faith creates hindrances to reaching our final destination successfully.

> It is impossible to please God without faith. Anyone who wants to come to him must believe that there is a God and that he rewards those who sincerely seek him.
> —Hebrews 11:6

Many of us in the body of Christ do not realize that faith cannot work where sin abides. At times we pray and we believe God is not answering; however, the reason we may not receive the answer we want is that He sees sin in our hearts. I am talking about those little things we might not consider sinful, such as being unforgiving, being judgmental, or perhaps harboring some form of prejudice toward others. These are the kinds of acts we deem to be little, but God sees them differently. We might not consider this to have any relevance for us today, but I assure you it does. God hates sin not only on a personal level but also as it relates to a nation! There is no such thing as a small sin. Sin is sin, and it causes us to lose the blessing.

There are two vital lessons we should consider when dealing with our own sin. First, it is essential that we deal with sin immediately and repent of any transgressions. We need to recognize our wrongdoing and ask God for forgiveness. Second, before moving forward, wait for guidance and direction from the Lord. It is impossible for us to win any of life's battles without His guidance. It might appear that we have a great life and that things are under control and managed in accordance with what our puny minds consider to be success, but it takes a great deal of patience and determination to wait on the Lord. When we do, the journey to our final destination will be beyond successful. During your next encounter with adversity, consider seeking wisdom from the Lord before proceeding. If the Lord made a promise, do not allow impatience to cause you to step ahead of His plan. When we have renewed our minds with direction from the Guidebook for life, things flow according to the will of God.

INNER TRANSFORMATION

Our sinful nature is something we all came into the world with. The nature was given to all through one man, Adam. Another man, Jesus, entered the world and redeemed mankind from sin by giving us the Holy Spirit. Through the Cross, Jesus delivered us from sin. Yet many absolutely refuse to accept this gift. The gift of redemption from sin and a life of freedom from bondage is the most extraordinary gift humanity will ever receive.

The only way to have a cleared and renewed mind is to have a heart aligned to righteousness. When we trust Jesus Christ as our personal Savior, the power of sin in our lives is broken. However, our distaste for sin does not just go away overnight. The menace within us, our flesh, keeps us entangled with sin. Sin does to the psyche what fog does to the freeway—it makes us unable to see clearly, and we end up driving blindly. Without a renewal of the mind, we will continue to emulate the behavior of the world instead of that of the kingdom.

> Don't copy the behavior and customs of this world, but let God transform you into a new person by changing the way you think. Then you will know what God wants you to do, and you will know how good and pleasing and perfect his will really is.
>
> —ROMANS 12:2

To successfully achieve our objective of mind renewal, there are some adjustments we must make to our thought pattern. As I thought about the topic, there is a quote from Ira Gassen that clearly reflects what I would like to get across. It states, "Be careful of your thoughts; they may become words at any moment."[2] Many of us are where we are because of the way we think, the words we speak, the people with whom we have encircled ourselves, and the goals we have outlined. Become aware of the things to which you pay attention. Are you more interested in watching all the negativity on the news—the shooting, the abuse, and the gossip—or are you more interested in people helping and caring about each other? Negative conversations open the door for darkness to enter your sphere. Purpose yourself to think positive thoughts, and like words will follow. The end result of taking this one step will reveal itself in as little as thirty days in the form of a peace that surpasses all understanding. When we realize that we have a choice of where and upon what we cast our eyes, we will choose the light of God. What we look at affects our mind. It is the mind that affects the world outside of us.

Today, pay attention to what is allowed to get into your mind. If we were able to see what God sees in us, we would all do the right things. To renew the psyche requires that we cling to belief in Jesus as the only Person with the power to renew our mind supernaturally. When we accept the offer of salvation, we change from independence, living for ourselves, to dependence on the Spirit of God within us. Renewal of the mind and spirit is the key to a successful life in God.

> Now, the Lord is the Spirit, and wherever the Spirit of the Lord is,
> he gives freedom.
> —2 Corinthians 3:17

After salvation, God intended for mankind to experience a transformation or metamorphosis, much like that of a caterpillar into a butterfly. However, the metamorphosis process from caterpillar to butterfly is an involuntary one for the species, because they are lacking the free will that has been given to man. Mankind is the only species in the Earth's realm with free will. Fortunately for the caterpillar, it pretty much lives in accordance to the will of God. They are pretty much forced to be in total surrender to the Creator, which is a very good thing. Caterpillars do not backslide; they continue on the path given, unlike mankind.

One of the greatest experiences of change is to commit to accomplishing the desired outcome. When it comes to learning about permanent changes in our lives, we can learn a great deal from the caterpillar. Mind renewal is about a total and complete makeover. The essence of any change begins with a blueprint. Fortunately for believers, we have the ability to commit to a complete, voluntary surrender to the will of God. The more we come to the clear understanding of who Christ is in us and who we are in Him, the more we are able to respond in extraordinary ways. As we walk with Him in faith and not by sight, we will soar as high as an eagle. We will experience metamorphosis with a change in our character.

When the input of the seed of God's Word becomes whole and complete on the inside of our heart, the full manifestation of metamorphosis is revealed on the outside. If we use the example of the caterpillar to butterfly as the target, believers also require cocoon time to meditate and rejuvenate. The cocoon provides a haven away from the world system.

> So I tell you, don't worry about everyday life—whether you have enough food, drink, and clothes. Doesn't life consist of more than food and clothing? Look at the birds. They don't need to plant or harvest or put food in barns because your heavenly Father feeds them. And you are far more valuable to him than they are. Can all your worries add a single moment to your life? Of course not.
>
> —Matthew 6:25–27

Let's commit to a renewal of our mind by replacing some of your current entertainment activities with the Word of God. Like the butterfly, the light of God's Word will transform your inner being to reflect the outer glory of the God within you. Our Creator has indicated that before splendor occurs there is always a struggle. Your assignment is to have faith, be patient, and trust that the Holy Spirit will manifest an outer mind renewal from your commitment to the inner, daily input of God's Word.

There are so many distractions that can keep us from renewing our mind. The process requires a great deal of focus and commitment. When we ignore the need to focus on our thoughts, it affects all other steps in the journey. If we are not in a place of mind renewal, we worry. When we worry, we say to God, "I do not believe or trust You to do what You promised to do." What we need to realize is that whenever we receive a promise from God, bet your life on it, for it shall come to pass. When confronted with adversity we can wallow in the sadness or we can choose to confront the situation and develop from the experience. The adversity which ultimately led me to the end result of the book was the peril of unemployment. I turned to God. I made Him the Source. He then became responsible for the outcome.

> Without wavering, let us hold tightly to the hope we say we have,
> for God can be trusted to keep his promise.
> —Hebrew 10:23

The Word of God will successfully give you the triumph over every experience of peril in your life. The prerequisite is faith, coupled with obedience, trust, and uttering the right words.

Words Create Our Final Destination

> And the tongue is a flame of fire. It is full of wickedness that can
> ruin your whole life. It can turn the entire course of your life into a
> blazing flame of destruction, for it is set on fire by hell itself.
> —James 3:6

Words are very powerful. They shape the end result of every single experience in our lives. In order to receive blessing from the words we speak, we need to speak God's words. How do we communicate? Words. How do we transfer our thoughts? Words. Words are used to communicate our thoughts and to assist the listener in perceiving the same message. Words have a tremendous impact on our destiny. When we accept God's Word as the full authority over our life—and then when we do the Word—we become eligible to be partakers of the heavenly inheritance (Heb. 3:1).

> Pay attention, my child, to what I say. Listen carefully. Don't lose
> sight of my words. Let them penetrate deep within your heart, for
> they bring life and radiant health to anyone who discovers their
> meaning. Above all else, guard your heart, for it affects everything
> you do. Avoid all perverse talk; stay far from corrupt speech. Look
> straight ahead, and fix your eyes on what lies before you. Mark out
> a straight path for your feet; then stick to the path and stay safe.
> Don't get sidetracked; keep your feet from following evil.
> —Proverb 4:20–27

Words heal us or make us sick, and they are able to bless or curse us. Think about this scenario: Someone asked for prayer for healing. While people pray the Word of God for healing as requested—"[Jesus] took our sicknesses and removed our diseases" (Matt. 8:17)—the sick person continuously murmurs, "I know I will never get better." This person, by saying these words, can rest assured that they will not be healed. This behavior is quite common among many believers, for they are unaware that their words create their reality.

Jesus only spoke the end result, and He has also given us the authority to manifest what the Word says. Many believers do not have faith that their prayers will be answered. Without faith, nothing changes. Our words should be chosen with care, as our lives will be influenced by them positively or negatively. It is crucial to make words work to bring about the desired end result in our lives. Our entire atmosphere is a product of words.

> In the beginning the Word already existed. He was with God, and he was God. He was in the beginning with God. He created everything there is. Nothing exists that he didn't make. Life itself was in him, and this life gives light to everyone.
> —JOHN 1:1–4

> Then God said, "Let there be light," and there was light!
> —GENESIS 1:3

An important principle of truth is the use of words to create your heart's desires. Are your words aligned with those of our Creator? Use spoken words to manifest successful end results. Many of us are speaking in complete opposition to the will of God. We break the covenant when we speak outside of the guidelines. Here is an example of the words that we invite to take up residence in our lives: "I am so old." "I come from a family with heart disease, so most likely I have inherited it." "I am too fat." "I am afraid." "I am broke." "I am so sick." "These shoes are killing me." Have you ever visited a sick person? Pay attention to the conversation, specifically the words they utter. The body of Christ is most guilty of this issue with speaking contrary to God's will.

God's words have creative power in them. As believers, we have been given authority to speak our end results. Hence, when we get up in the morning, instead of leaving our day to chance we should surrender our mind, will, emotion, consciousness, and spirit to the will of God. This is a prayer that I use daily that you may want to consider. Before I get out of bed, I say, "Holy Spirit, I make myself available to You. I forsake my thoughts for Yours. Only allow me to speak, see, and hear what's coming from You. Jesus, reveal Yourself boldly in me. I am determined to seek God with all of my heart. Help me day by day to develop a faith that will never waiver. In Jesus' name I pray. Amen!"

> The tongue can kill or nourish life.
> —PROVERBS 18:21

Speak only God's Word!

The Key to Continual Peace

What is prayer? It is a conversation with our heavenly Father and our greatest time saver. Scripture makes it clear that God hears and answers prayers. Jesus assured us that if we prayed in line with God's will and in the name of Jesus, He will answer our prayers.

> One day Jesus told his disciples a story to illustrate their need for constant prayer and to show them that they must never give up.
> —Luke 18:1

There are two truths that I discovered that changed my life forever. The first is the truth of the gospel of Jesus Christ. Second, I learned that prayer without faith and outside of the will of God accomplishes nothing.

> Listen to me! You can pray for anything, and if you believe, you will have it. But when you are praying, first forgive anyone you are holding a grudge against, so that your Father in heaven will forgive your sins, too.
> —Mark 11:24–25

Prayer is the key determinant of where we end up in life and how much time it takes us to get there. We are all governed by a ticking clock. Jesus was always interested in time; however, He knew that His Father provided the appropriate amount of time to accomplish the will assigned. Many of us in the body of Christ say, "I just do not have time to make God and prayer a priority." There will always be competing concerns in our lives, but when we place our personal relationship with God first, He becomes responsible for the outcome.

Jesus started His ministry at the age of thirty, which means He had just over one thousand days to perform the most miraculous, far-reaching accomplishment of anyone in human history. Jesus' ministry was done as man, not deity. If Jesus had performed His earthly ministry because He was God, then you and I could not follow His example, because we are not God. However, we can minister as Jesus did because we have His same Spirit, His Holy Spirit. We are a part of Jesus' "greater works," but we need to be connected to His Holy Spirit to partake of the blessing.

God, in His omniscience, knew exactly how much time Jesus needed to complete the assignment in the Earth's realm. Likewise, He knows the amount of time each believer needs daily to accomplish His will in their

lives when His tool is used. If we love God, there is no real explanation for
not having time to give Him priority in prayer and guidance.

Jesus is our Blueprint and our Anchor. Keep in mind, God created each
and every one of us and made us in His own image.

> The truth is, anyone who believes in me will do the same works I
> have done, and even greater works, because I am going to be with
> the Father.
>
> —JOHN 14:12

God knows the beginning, middle, and end. His Word represents righteousness. Therefore, for a follower of Jesus Christ to make lack of time
the reason to forsake an intimate, personal relationship with Him is a dis-
service to oneself. God has given us the Guidebook. However, we have
neglected to take it seriously enough to implement in our lives.

Keep in mind that we have been given access and authority over all in the
Earth's realm. However, we must adhere to the rules of the kingdom. Once
we learn this, we are on track to tap into successful end results. Without
prayer our end results will never be aligned with those of our Creator.
Ignoring God is not going to avoid life's ultimate question, where we will
spend eternity.

> The earnest prayer of a righteous person has great power and won-
> derful results. Elijah was as human as we are, and yet when he
> prayed earnestly that no rain would fall, none fell for the next three
> and a half years! Then he prayed for rain, and down it poured. The
> grass turned green, and the crops began to grow again.
>
> —JAMES 5:16–18

BE PREPARED FOR THE END RESULT

⑪

T IS NOT our worldly education, wealth, or influence that makes us successful. It is how we allow the Spirit of God to guide us and what we allow Him to do through us. Once you pursue a personal, intimate relationship with your Creator, you will be astounded as to what He is able to do in you. My heart aches for those who have followed the world's defiant ways and forsaken the God of the universe. The only treasure we can take to heaven is our soul! Be watchful and prepared, for He could be on His way today. Will He know you?

My brother died suddenly on December 4, 2012, as I was preparing to release my manuscript to the publisher. He was prepared for that final destination. My tribute to him was as follows.

> Today, I find myself in a place of peace that surpasses all understanding. That peace comes from my awareness of Toni's spiritual development. In 2009 during a week-long study of the Word of God at a believer's conference we attended together, Toni discerned that this journey was not one of religion but one of relationship development with our Creator. Toni further discovered that he had a blood covenant with God and that it was way bigger than being saved and saying, "I am a Christian." He realized that just as we develop relationships with people we would like to know better, the same principal should be applied to developing an intimate, personal relationship with God. So his pursuit commenced back then.
>
> Since God is Spirit, the relationship with God has to be developed in the spirit with His Word. We all are spirits living in a body. Since we are all made in the image of God, whether we believe in Him or not we are also spirits.
>
> Toni was at a point in his spiritual development that he knew that time was of the essence. In this journey, every day that passes we are all inching closer to that predestined appointment, our final, eternal destination, where we will come face to face with

our Maker. There is absolutely nothing that will exempt us from this appointment—not wealth, not higher education, not friends in high places, not professional accomplishment, prominent positions, nor a high level of earthly authority.

The major reason why there are so many unhappy people in the world is that we are seeking happiness in relationships with mere men and outside of God. God created us to be in relationship with Him, and in our rebellion we have missed the most extraordinary oneness possible.

We always blame God when things go wrong, but remember He gave us free will. We have no right to blame Him for anything if we have not taken the time to read and study the Guidebook, which reveals His ways. Here is what He tells us in His Word:

My people are destroyed because they don't know me.

—HOSEA 4:6

Mostly we destroy ourselves because we don't know God.

It does not get any better than an intimate, personal relationship with our Creator. Toni achieved success where it mattered most in the eternal and in God. Toni activated his spirit man in faith and belief. Well done, Toni. You truly received the eternal message of the gospel of the good news of Jesus and His offer of salvation through His death, burial, and resurrection.

Had I not been close to my brother, I would have not known about his eternal readiness. Instead, I would have been in a state of unrest. Are you prepared for that final destination? We have been given a reference as to what our final destination would look like in God's Word.

The Kingdom of Heaven can be illustrated by the story of ten bridesmaids who took their lamps and went to meet the bridegroom. Five of them were foolish, and five were wise. The five who were foolish took no oil for their lamps, but the other five were wise enough to take along extra oil. When the bridegroom was delayed, they all lay down and slept. At midnight they were roused by the shout, "Look, the bridegroom is coming! Come out and welcome him!" All the bridesmaids got up and prepared their lamps. Then the five foolish ones asked the others, "Please give us some of your oil because our lamps are going out." But the others replied, "We don't have enough for all of us. Go to a shop and buy some for yourselves." But while they were gone to buy oil, the bridegroom came, and those who were ready went in with him to the marriage feast, and the door was locked. Later, when the other five bridesmaids returned, they stood outside, calling, "Sir, open the door for us!" But he called back, "I don't know you!" So stay awake and be prepared, because you do not know the day or hour of my return.

—Matthew 25:1–13

Who Are We?

Until we find the answer to this question we will never discover our purpose on the Earth. It is very unfortunate that many of us believe that self-discovery is accomplished through receiving validation from other human beings. According to the Word of God, we are made in His image and were created for a specific purpose to accomplish His will for humanity. Our being should be modeled from His existence. However, because of our fallen nature, we lack the ability to know God apart from His willingness to reveal Himself. Man's logic will never identify God. Therefore, mere man will never be able to know our Creator unless He chooses to reveal Himself.

Are you living life thoughtlessly? When we sacrifice eternity for the pleasure of the moment, we are living recklessly.

And how do you benefit if you gain the whole world but lose your own soul in the process?

—Luke 9:25

The only security available to mankind in the Earth's realm that leads into eternity is salvation received by the grace of God. Our Creator has given every person the free will to activate the Spirit of God or allow it to remain dormant. We can go through defeat in our health, wealth, and relationships; however, if we have never tapped in to the free gift of the Spirit and resurrection power offered to all of humanity by way of salvation, we have missed the essence of creation and what life is all about. Contrary to popular belief, a relationship with the Holy Spirit inside us is a prerequisite to create that inner peace and eventual eternal life we all seek. Invest in your spiritual life now. Development widens our ability to accept and enjoy God's grace instantaneously.

If you do this, you will experience God's peace, which is far more wonderful than the human mind can understand. His peace will guard your hearts and minds as you live in Christ Jesus.

—Philippians 4:7

God said in His Word, "If you want me to protect you, learn to believe what I say" (Isa. 7:9). Would you like to recognize God's voice? God wants us to know Him intimately. Why?

> "For I know the plans I have for you," says the LORD. "They are plans for good and not for disaster, to give you a future and a hope. In those days when you pray, I will listen. If you look for me in earnest, you will find me when you seek me."
> —JEREMIAH 29:11–13

I challenge you to pursue an intimate, personal relationship with God. It is accomplished in the same manner human closeness develops—with a time commitment. The Bible is not just a mere book. It is a message from the Creator of the universe to humanity and the only source available to develop intimacy with Him. Do you have the courage to trust God in an intimate relationship? Mere man disappoints, but God's Word does what He says it will do. This is a message of the hidden wealth in God's grace; money cannot buy it, and death is unable to take it away. The onus is on all believers to pursue the most valuable relationship in the Earth's realm. It is my hope that after reading this book divine truth will propel you to take the next step to create intimacy with the Creator of the universe.

> Friendship with the LORD is reserved for those who fear him. With them he shares the secrets of his covenant.
> —PSALM 25:14

We cannot conquer perils in our lives peacefully without the use of the Guidebook with instructions for life in the Earth's realm.

> Human plans, no matter how wise or well advised, cannot stand against the LORD.
> —PROVERBS 21:30

The highest form of wisdom known to man is to know the mind of God, which is discerned in intimacy with Him.

> "Should I hide my plan from Abraham?" the LORD asked.
> —GENESIS 18:17

NOTES

CHAPTER 1:
THE BIBLE IS OUR WEAPON AGAINST ADVERSITY

1.   *Dictionary.com*, s.v. "weapon," accessed July 13, 2014, at http://dictionary.reference.com/browse/weapon.

2.   Excerpts from this address may be found at "225 Years Ago Today...," *An Act of Mind*, 30 Apr., 2014, accessed July 13, 2014, at http://anactofmind.com/category/religious-freedom/.

3.   George Washington, Inaugural Address of 1789, available at *National Archives and Records Administration*, accessed July 17, 2014, at http://www.archives.gov/exhibits/american_originals/inaugtxt.html.

4.   This quote comes from a letter John Adams wrote to his wife, Abigail, when they first moved into the White House in 1800. It may be found at *TheWhiteHouseMuseum.org*, accessed July 18, 2014, at http://www.whitehousemuseum.org/floor1/state-dining-room.htm.

5.   John Adams, *Papers of John Adams, Vol. 1–2* (Boston, MA: Belknap Press, 2003, 126, accessed at Google Books online, July 18, 2014, at http://books.google.com/books?id=j3CgEwKTcG8C&printsec=frontcover#v=onepage&q&f=false.

6.   Constitution of Massachusetts of 1780, accessed at The National Humanities Institute Online, July 19, 2014, at http://www.nhinet.org/ccs/docs/ma-1780.htm.

7.   Quoted at Monticello.org, accessed July 19, 2014, at http://www.monticello.org/site/jefferson/quotations-jefferson-memorial.

8.   Ibid.

9.   Quoted in William Eleroy Curtis, *The True Thomas Jefferson* (Southaven, MS: Booker House Publishing Company, 2013), 337, accessed at Google Books, July 20, 2014.

10.   Quoted in Steve Coffman, *Words of the Founding Fathers* (Jefferson, NC: McFarland, 2012), 41, accessed at Google Books.

11.   This quote is excerpted from Benjamin Franklin's address during the Constitutional Convention of 1787. A transcript of that address is available at "Benjamin Franklin's Request for Prayers at the Constitutional Convention," *BeliefNet*, accessed July 13, 2014, at http://www.beliefnet.com/resourcelib/docs/21/Benjamin_Franklins_Request_for_Prayers_at_the_Constitutional__1.html.

12.   This quote and others available at "Benjamin Franklin," *Our Republic Online*, accessed July 13, 2014, at http://www.ourrepubliconline.com/Author/21.

13.   This quote and others available at "Benjamin Franklin," *Conservative Forum*, accessed July 13, 2014, at http://www.conservativeforum.org/authquot.asp?ID=2.

14.   "James A. Garfield—The Brokered Convention President," *The Conservative Treehouse*, accessed July 13, 2014, at http://theconservativetreehouse .com/2012/03/08/james-a-garfield-the-brokered-convention-president/.

Chapter 3:
God Promises to Be the Source for All Our Needs

1.   This quote may be found at "Helen Keller Quotes," *ThinkExist.com*, accessed July 14, 2014, at http://thinkexist.com/quotation/when_one_door_of_ happiness_closes-another_opens/144271.html.

Chapter 4:
The Number One Resource to Conquer Perils

1.   *Dictionary.com*, s.v. "extraordinary," accessed July 18, 2014, at http:// dictionary.reference.com/browse/most+extraordinary.

2.   "William Tyndale," *ChristianityToday.com*, accessed July 18, 2014, at http://www.christianitytoday.com/ch/131christians/scholarsandscientists/ tyndale.html.

3.   "Martin Luther," *Biography.com*, accessed July 17, 2014, at http://www .biography.com/people/martin-luther-9389283.

4.   Derek Suderman, "Luther's Beliefs," *Global Mennonite Anabaptist Encyclopedia Online*, accessed July 15, 2014, at http://www.mhsc.ca/index .php?content=http://www.mhsc.ca/mennos/bluther.html.

5.   Henry Madison Morris, *Men of Science, Men of God: Great Scientists Who Believed the Bible* (Green Forest, AR: Master Books, 2007).

6.   "George Washington Carver and Other Christians Who Were Scientists," Georgia Southern University Online, accessed July 14, 2014, at https://sites.google.com/a/georgiasouthern.edu/etmcmull/george-washington -carver-and-other-christians-who-were-scientists.

Chapter 5:
Order Your Steps

1.   *Dictionary.com*, s.v. "religion," accessed July 14, 2014, at http://dictionary .reference.com/browse/religion.

2.   Ibid., s.v. "intimacy," accessed July 14, 2014, http://dictionary.reference .com/browse/relationship?s=t.

3.   Frank Newport, "Just Why Do Americans Attend Church?" *Gallup*, 6 April, 2007, accessed July 15, 2014, at http://www.gallup.com/poll/27124/ just-why-americans-attend-church.aspx.

4.   *Dictionary.com*, s.v., "oppressed," accessed July 13, 2014, at http:// dictionary.reference.com/browse/oppress?s=t.

5.   *Dictionary.com*, s.v., "tithe," accessed July 14, 2014, at http://dictionary .reference.com/browse/tithe?s=t.

Chapter 8:
In Surrender God Is Our Companion

1. *Dictionary.com*, s.v. "surrender," accessed July 14, 2014, at http://dictionary.reference.com/browse/surrender?s=t.

Chapter 9:
Who Is Leading You?

1. *Dictionary.com*, s.v. "baptism," accessed July 15, 2014, at http://dictionary.reference.com/browse/baptism.

Chapter 10:
Discover Your True Journey

1. Ibid., s.v. "freedom."
2. Ira Gassen quote may be found at "Ira Gassen," *ThinkExist.com*, accessed July 17, 2014, at http://thinkexist.com/quotes/ira_gassen/.

ABOUT THE AUTHOR

Lorna Lumpris discovered her divine inheritance during an extended chapter of adversity in her life. She sought after answers to her quandary in the Instruction Book for life. This is a book available to all and provides direction for successful living in the Earth's realm to those who use it. Her passion to know more led to a commitment to the precepts in the Instruction Book. In 2006, she experienced an encounter with the Creator of all things that would change her life completely.

Lorna received a message from the Creator of all things in July 2011 to write the book *Perils of Life*. In obedience to His call, she completed the assignment with guidance from the Holy Spirit.